MR. LINCOLN'S
HIGH-TECH WAR

A new tool of war carries soldiers' eyes aloft.

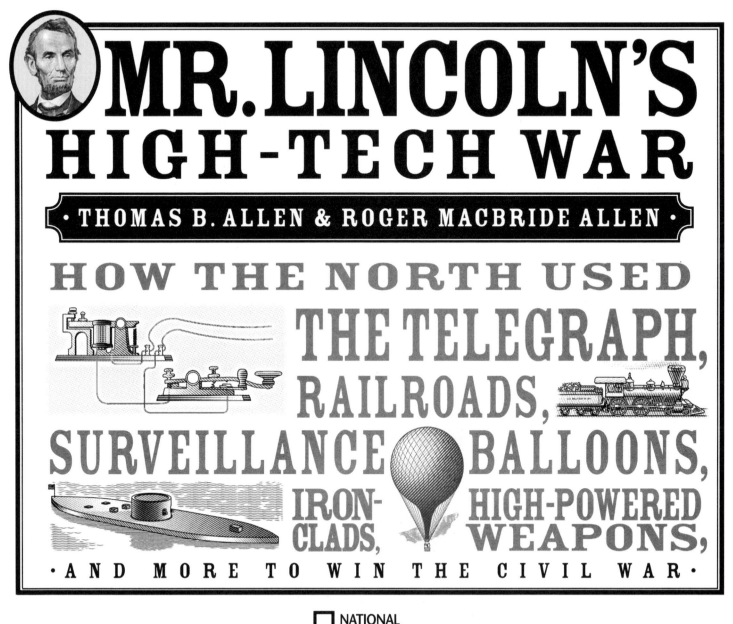

MR. LINCOLN'S HIGH-TECH WAR

· THOMAS B. ALLEN & ROGER MACBRIDE ALLEN ·

HOW THE NORTH USED **THE TELEGRAPH, RAILROADS,** SURVEILLANCE **BALLOONS,** IRON-CLADS, **HIGH-POWERED WEAPONS,** · AND MORE TO WIN THE CIVIL WAR ·

NATIONAL GEOGRAPHIC
WASHINGTON, D.C.

More information about the topics in this book
as well as on the Civil War in general can be found
at this book's Web site:
www.mrlincolnshightechwar.com

For information about special discounts for bulk
purchases, please contact
National Geographic Books Special Sales:
ngspecsales@ngs.org

For rights or permissions inquiries, please contact
National Geographic Books Subsidiary Rights:
ngbookrights@ngs.org

Cover design by Bea Jackson and David M. Seager.
Book design by David M. Seager.
Text is set in Celestia Antiqua.
Display type is Rosewood Filled.

Library of Congress Cataloging-in-Publication Data

Allen, Thomas B.
Mr. Lincoln's high-tech war : how the North used the
telegraph, railroads, surveillance balloons, ironclads,
high-powered weapons, and more to win the Civil War
/ by Thomas B. Allen and Roger MacBride Allen.
    p. cm.
Includes bibliographical references and index.
ISBN 978-1-4263-0379-1 (hardcover : alk. paper)
ISBN 978-1-4263-0380-7 (library binding : alk. paper)
1. United States—History—Civil War, 1861–1865—
Technology. 2. United States. Army—History—Civil
War, 1861–1865. 3. Lincoln, Abraham, 1809–1865.
4. Technology—United States—History—19th century.
I. Allen, Roger MacBride. II. Title.
E468.9.A44 2008
973.7'301—dc22

                                      2008024546

Printed in the United States of America

· CONTENTS ·

The new age of invention, captured in this print by Currier & Ives, inspired young Abraham Lincoln. As President, he transformed railroads, the telegraph, and steam-powered ships into high-tech weapons of war.

· THE SPIRIT OF INVENTION ·

In 1809 Abraham Lincoln was born into the last generation of Americans who did not expect technology ever to change. Young Abraham lived, with the rest of his family, in a series of dirt-floor cabins in Kentucky, Indiana, and Illinois. Those cabins, the farm implements, the guns used for hunting, all the cooking utensils, and everything else the family owned would have seemed quite familiar to Abraham's father, his grand-father, and his father before him—and not all that differ-ent from the things that Abraham's great-great-great-great-grandfather Samuel Lincoln might have used at the time he arrived in America from England in 1637. Samuel would have instantly recognized and known how to use nearly all the tools and farm implements that young Abraham would have worked with in the 1810s and 1820s. Even the flintlock gun in the Lincoln

As a boy, Lincoln lived in a log cabin like this.

cabin wouldn't have changed all that much in the last 150 years.

But Abraham's own father, Thomas Lincoln, would have been dumbfounded by the railroad, the steamboat, the telegraph, and the dozens of other inventions that came boiling out of inventors' workshops in the early years of the 19th century.

By the start of the 1800s, technology had already begun to transform work, transportation, education, and other parts of life for Americans. The Industrial Revolution was well underway in England while Abraham Lincoln was growing up, and it would change the lives of millions of people around the world in the years to come.

As a father, Lincoln wanted to show his five-year-old son Robert what technology was bringing to America. So, one day in 1848 Lincoln, at the time a first-term U.S. Congressman from Illinois, walked with Robert up the

☞ TO FIND MORE INFORMATION ABOUT SUBJECTS IN THIS BOOK AS WELL AS THE CIVIL WAR IN GENERAL, VISIT THIS BOOK'S WEB SITE: www.mrlincolnshightechwar.com ☜

broad steps of the Patent Office Building. In the Model Room, they saw small-scale versions of ideas. The little machines and gadgets looked like toys to Robert.

At that time, inventors had to send the Patent Office models of their inventions. After examiners looked over a model and decided that it demonstrated a new idea, they would give it a patent. This allowed the inventor to be the only person with the right to own and sell that invention.

A while after Lincoln and Robert visited the Patent Office, Lincoln was aboard a river steamboat that ran aground and had to struggle to get underway again. The mishap gave him an idea for a device that could be attached to the sides of a ship. Filling it with air would lift the ship and allow it to float over a shallow stretch of water.

He began whittling a model that he took to a lawyer who specialized in patents. The lawyer prepared the necessary papers and sent them, with the model, to the Patent Office. On May 22, 1849, the model earned Abraham Lincoln Patent Number 6469 for "A Device for Buoying Vessels Over Shoals." Lincoln is the only President ever to be granted a patent.

Lincoln understood the importance of inventions—and patents like his—to the country. Patents, he said, "secured to the inventor, for a limited time, the exclusive use of his invention; and thereby added the fuel of interest to the fire of genius, in the discovery and production of new and useful things."

Decades later, as President during the Civil War, he would see the military importance of the telegraph and railroads and many other "new and useful things" long before his generals did. Lincoln became the first U.S. President to step fully into the role of Commander in Chief in wartime. Within six months of taking office, he took control of the North's railroads and telegraph lines, introduced aerial surveillance to the Union army, urged the production of advanced weaponry, ordered the building of ironclad ships, and began a naval blockade that strangled the South's economy.

The Civil War was the climax of a struggle between free states and slave states that had been going on for a bloodstained decade. When Lincoln became President, that struggle would be his to finish, once and for all.

1850-1860:
· A NATION MOVING TOWARD CIVIL WAR ·

1850

● Congress passes the Fugitive Slave Act, aimed at stopping the flight of slaves to the North by making it illegal for anyone to help a slave escape from a master.

1854

● A law introduced by Senator Stephen A. Douglas of Illinois threatens the balance between the Union's slave and free states by letting people in the Kansas Territory vote on whether to allow slavery in their future state.

● In "Bleeding Kansas," abolitionists (people opposed to slavery) fight pro-slavers, many of them armed border-crossers from Missouri. One of the abolitionists is Connecticut-born John Brown.

● The Republican Party is formed in opposition to the Douglas-sponsored law, which wipes out the Missouri Compromise. Republicans, opposing expansion of slavery, defeat many Democrats in Congressional elections.

1856

● Brown and his followers, including four of his sons, kill five pro-slavers in Kansas as he begins a crusade to free all slaves.

1857

● The U.S. Supreme Court, under Chief Justice Roger Taney, rules seven to two against Dred Scott, a slave who said he ought to be freed because he had lived in free states. The Court says Scott had no right to go to court because black people could not be U.S. citizens and thus "had no rights which the white man was bound to respect."

1858

● Illinois Republicans nominate Lincoln to oppose Democrat Douglas in the U.S. Senate race. In a campaign speech Lincoln says, "A house divided against itself cannot stand. I believe this government cannot endure permanently half slave and half free."

1859

● The Illinois legislature chooses Douglas for the U.S. Senate over Lincoln by a vote of 54 to 46. (Not until the 17th Amendment is ratified in 1913 will the U.S. Constitution call for the election of Senators by a vote of the people rather than by the state legislature.)

● John Brown, leading 21 men (16 whites and 5 African Americans), raids the federal arsenal at Harpers Ferry, Virginia, planning to arm slaves for his crusade. Federal soldiers and Marines, under the command of U.S. Army Lieutenant Colonel Robert E. Lee, wound Brown and kill most of his men, including two of his sons.

● Convicted of treason against Virginia, John Brown is hanged. Before he is executed, he predicts that "the crimes of this guilty land will never be purged away, but with Blood."

1860

● Lincoln, chosen by Republicans as their candidate for President, begins his campaign, running against Democrat Douglas, Southern Democrat John C. Breckinridge, and John Bell of the Constitution Union Party.

● Lincoln is elected President on November 6. Beginning on December 20, Southern states vote to secede from (leave) the United States and begin the process of forming the Confederate States of America.

● Southern Congressmen begin resigning and heading home to support the Confederacy.

● Outgoing President James Buchanan, who has Southern sympathies, denies the right of states to secede but believes that the federal government does not have the legal power to stop them.

A poster for the 1860 election campaign shows the Republican Party candidates for President and Vice President. Hannibal Hamlin, a longtime Maine politician, agreed with Lincoln's feelings about slavery.

CHAPTER ONE

· LINCOLN'S SECRET TRAIN ·

On election night, November 6, 1860, Abraham Lincoln crouched by a clattering telegraph key in Springfield, Illinois, listening to the dots and dashes of Morse code that carried reports on the voting. Not until early the next morning did he learn that he had been elected. He had 1,865,593 popular votes, compared to the combined 2,823,975 votes of his three opponents. He received a majority or plurality of the vote in 17 states—none of them in the South. The 180 electoral votes gave him the election. His opponents' combined electoral vote was 123.

He was President-elect of a divided nation gripped by fear of civil war. He would not take the oath of office and begin serving as President until March 4, 1861. But for him, the war had already begun. Two days after learning

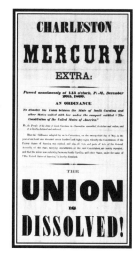

Charleston gets the news about secession.

he had been elected, he read a newspaper dispatch that said a dummy made up to look like him had been hanged by a mob in Pensacola, Florida. It would be the first of many threats against his life. On December 20, South Carolina seceded, beginning the withdrawal of Southern states from the Union.

Everyone knew that President-elect Lincoln would journey to his Inauguration in Washington by train from Springfield. This was the modern way to travel, a demonstration of how railroads could tie together a nation geographically even as it was being torn apart politically. Only four years before, the first railroad bridge across the Mississippi River had been completed. People could travel from New York to eastern Iowa in just 42 hours!

His journey from Springfield to Washington began

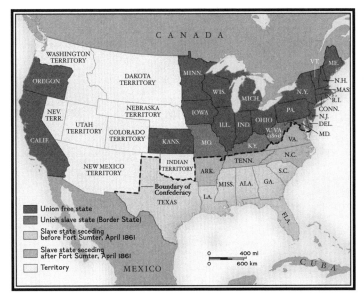

This map of secession shows the states that made up the Confederacy, south of the dashed line.

on February 11. Eager to promote pro-Union sentiment, Lincoln planned a 1,904-mile train ride that would take 12 days, with time out for him to give several speeches and make many appearances along the way. But Allan Pinkerton, the nation's most famous private detective, would change Lincoln's plans.

Pinkerton's major clients were railroad companies. The country's trains were like little cities without police as they passed from one stop to the next, their passengers, mail, and freight unprotected. If criminals robbed a train, the railroad got no help from either the federal government or the state through which the train was traveling. Pinkerton supplied operatives to keep watch over trains and track down robbers. Early in 1861, acting on a tip from a railroad executive, the private detective learned of a plot to kill the President-elect in Baltimore.

Maryland, reacting to Lincoln's election, was teetering between North and South. The plotters were secessionists—supporters of the idea that states could secede from (leave) the Union. They planned to strike as Lincoln rode in a horse-drawn carriage through Baltimore. While some of them staged a riot, a barber who called himself Captain Cipriano Ferrandini would kill Lincoln, disappear into the mob, and make his way to a hero's welcome somewhere in the South. Baltimore's mayor and chief of police, both of whom were pro-South, would see to it that there were few policemen around when the riot began.

The secessionists intended to cut off rail and telegraph connections between Baltimore and Washington,

Cartoonists imagined all sorts of disguises Lincoln could have used to enter Washington on his secret train trip.

isolating the capital and putting it at risk for invasion from the South if war began. By the time Pinkerton started his investigation, Mississippi, Florida, Alabama, Georgia, Louisiana, and Texas had followed South Carolina out of the Union. "Civil war," said an Ohio newspaper, "is as certain to follow secession as darkness to follow the going down of the sun." After unearthing the Baltimore assassination plot, Pinkerton quickly set his own counterplot in motion.

Lincoln learned of the Baltimore conspiracy in Philadelphia on February 21, but he shrugged it off as just one of many death threats he had been told about. Then, he learned that word of the plot had also been heard in Washington by detectives hired by the U.S. Army to gather intelligence about secessionists in the capital city. Now Lincoln agreed to Pinkerton's plan to outwit the assassins.

The next morning, Lincoln participated in a flag-raising ceremony in front of Independence Hall. The 34th star on the flag recognized the admission of Kansas to the Union as a free state. Then he left for Harrisburg, as scheduled. After speaking before the state legislature, he and a bodyguard secretly boarded a special train back to Philadelphia. There, they were met by Pinkerton, who took them to the rail yard of the Philadelphia, Wilmington and Baltimore Railroad. Pinkerton also ordered the telegraph cut off between Philadelphia and Baltimore and put detectives in telegraph offices to stop the transmission of any messages mentioning Lincoln's travels.

Another Pinkerton agent, Kate Warne, met them at the train station. The nation's only female private eye, she had obtained tickets for herself, Pinkerton, the bodyguard, and Lincoln, describing the President-elect as her ailing brother. Instead of his usual stovepipe hat, he wore a slouch hat and tried to conceal his height by draping his overcoat around his shoulders. The three armed operatives accompanied Lincoln to a sleeping car, where he would be guarded. Shortly before 11 p.m., the train pulled out. When it arrived in Baltimore about 3:30 a.m. on February 23, the sleeping cars were uncoupled, shifted to other tracks, and then coupled to a Washington-bound train that arrived in the capital around 6 a.m. Lincoln was hurried out of the railroad station and into a carriage that took him to a hotel.

Samuel Morse Felton, the railroad president who had hired Pinkerton after hearing about the Baltimore plot, desperately wanted to know if the complex plan had worked. Using code names, Pinkerton telegraphed Felton: PLUMS [Pinkerton] DELIVERED NUTS [Lincoln] SAFELY.

Lincoln's arrival in Washington did not yet mean he had the reins of power. Because of the long delay between the November election and the March Inauguration, Lincoln had no legal authority to deal with the secession crisis that had been brewing since South Carolina left the Union.

The South Carolina state legislature had demanded that all federal property inside its borders be turned over to the state. The lawmakers refused to supply food to Fort Sumter, which stood on an island in Charleston Harbor. Major Robert Anderson, commander of the fort, and his soldiers found themselves in a trap. Unless the federal government could get them supplies, they would be forced to surrender.

By Inauguration Day on March 4, Washington was a city braced for war. Yet, surprisingly few soldiers were protecting the city. Most of the country's 16,000 soldiers were in Indian country, far beyond the reach of railroads. There were a few newly formed volunteer militias, but not all of them were loyal to the Union.

On the morning of the Inauguration, soldiers with rifles were at windows overlooking the Capitol's broad steps where Lincoln would take the oath of office. Troops lined the streets, and sharpshooters stood on rooftops along the route to the Capitol as Lincoln rode past in the traditional open carriage. Under the platform on which Lincoln stood to take the oath of office, other soldiers huddled, guarding against bomb planters. There were no incidents.

The next day, when President Lincoln walked into his

President Lincoln is Inaugurated on the steps of a Capitol that was getting a new dome. Work ended in 1863 when the Statue of Freedom topped the cast-iron dome.

White House office— what is now the Lincoln Bedroom (the first version of the Oval Office was not built until 1909)—the "very first thing placed in his hands" was a letter from the commander of the besieged Fort Sumter. Major Anderson and his men were running dangerously low on supplies and could not hold out much longer.

The President had to decide whether to surrender Fort Sumter to South Carolina or to send provisions to the fort and risk starting a civil war. Lincoln, ignoring his top general's advice to surrender, decided to send provisions. Only then did he discover the Union navy did not have the right ships for the job or any supplies ready. He sent a messenger to Charleston to inform South Carolina's governor that "an attempt will be made to supply Fort-Sumter with provisions only" and that if the attempt was not resisted, "no effort to throw in men, arms or ammunition, will be made"—except if there were to be an attack on the fort.

On April 12, 1861, long before Lincoln could sort out the problems of sending provisions, Confederate troops attacked the fort with cannon fire. The men in the fort fired back. The Civil War had begun.

*Cheering crowds send Massachusetts volunteers on their way to trains for their trip to
a worried Washington. People there feared invasion by Confederate troops.*

CHAPTER TWO

· LINCOLN TAKES COMMAND ·

Fort Sumter fell after 34 hours of Confederate cannon fire. The relief supplies Lincoln had planned to send had not yet even been loaded aboard ship. Lincoln declared a state of insurrection and called for 75,000 volunteers to enlist for 90 days of army service—the longest period he was allowed under a 1795 law that was still in force. Massachusetts, the first state to respond, sent men the fastest way possible: by train. The troops traveled as far as Philadelphia. There, volunteers from Pennsylvania—many of them without uniforms or weapons—boarded the cars. The next stop was Baltimore.

Baltimore was a busy, modern rail center where trains from five railroad companies converged. But old-time residents, clinging to their pre-rail memories, had passed

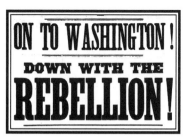

This rallying cry stirred Union volunteers to enlist.

local laws that prohibited noisy, smoke-belching trains from chugging through the center of the city. The Philadelphia, Wilmington and Baltimore Railroad, for example, ended its tracks on the east side of town, while the Baltimore and Ohio tracks stopped at a station at the far southern edge of the city. To transfer passengers who were continuing on, the two railroads disconnected cars from the locomotive and hitched them up to a team of horses that pulled the cars across the city on tracks laid in the street. (On Lincoln's trip to Washington, his car had been shunted this same way.)

The men from Massachusetts and Pennsylvania left Philadelphia early on the morning of April 19. On the way, Colonel Edward F. Jones, commanding the Sixth Massachusetts Regiment, feared that the train might be met by angry pro-South sympathizers. So, he ordered his men to

Rocks and clubs greet soldiers of the Sixth Massachusetts Regiment, fighting their way through Baltimore on the way to Washington.

load their weapons and "pay no attention to the mob, even if they throw stones, bricks, or other missiles; but if you are fired upon and any one of you is hit, your officers will order you to fire. Do not fire into any promiscuous crowds, but select any man whom you may see aiming at you, and be sure you drop him."

When the train arrived, nine of the horse-drawn cars transporting soldiers safely made the passage from one station to the other. Then, suddenly, a gang of secessionists, using stones, sand, and ships' anchors, blocked the rails. The rest of the soldiers now had to march through the streets to get to the other train. Members of the mob threw stones and bricks. Then came gunfire. Four soldiers were killed, the first of Lincoln's volunteers to die in the Civil War. The unarmed Pennsylvanians retreated and returned to Philadelphia while the Sixth Massachusetts Regiment made it to the other station and continued on to a panicky Washington.

Representatives from the Young Men's Christian Associations (YMCA) of Baltimore went to Washington to meet with Lincoln and urge him to make peace with the Confederacy. The YMCA delegates demanded that no more troops be sent through Maryland. Lincoln replied: "You would have me break my oath and surrender the Government without a blow....Our men are not moles, and cannot dig under the earth; they are not birds, and can't fly through the air. Go home and tell your people that if they will not attack us, we will not attack them; but if they do attack us, we will return it, and severely."

· "MARYLAND! MY MARYLAND!" ·

The confrontation that took place between Northern troops and Southern sympathizers at the train station in Baltimore inspired James Ryder Randall to write a poem titled "Maryland, My Maryland." The poem, which has been put to the music of "O Christmas Tree," has been the state's official song since 1939.

In the stanzas shown here, "despot" and "tyrant" are references to Abraham Lincoln. "Vandal" equates the Union army with the barbarian hordes that rampaged across Europe in the Middle Ages, and "Northern scum" is a term for the Sixth Massachusetts Regiment that traversed Baltimore. "[P]atriotic gore" refers to the death and injuries sustained by members of the mob when they attacked the Union forces.

I

The despot's heel is on thy shore,
Maryland! My Maryland!
His torch is at thy temple door,
Maryland! My Maryland!
Avenge the patriotic gore
That flecked the streets of
  Baltimore,
And be the battle queen of yore,
Maryland! My Maryland!

VI

Dear Mother! burst the tyrant's
  chain,
Maryland! My Maryland!
Virginia should not call in vain,
Maryland! My Maryland!
She meets her sisters on the
  plain—
"Sic semper!" 'tis the proud
  refrain
That baffles minions back amain,
Maryland! My Maryland!
Arise in majesty again,
Maryland! My Maryland!

VII

I see the blush upon thy cheek,
Maryland! My Maryland!
For thou wast ever bravely meek,
Maryland! My Maryland!
But lo! there surges forth a
  shriek,
From hill to hill, from creek to
  creek—
Potomac calls to Chesapeake,
Maryland! My Maryland!

VIII

Thou wilt not yield the Vandal
  toll,
Maryland! My Maryland!
Thou wilt not crook to his
  control,
Maryland! My Maryland!
Better the fire upon thee roll,
Better the blade, the shot, the
  bowl,
Than crucifixion of the soul,
Maryland! My Maryland!

A poem becomes a song.

IX

I hear the distant thunder-hum,
Maryland! My Maryland!
The Old Line's bugle, fife, and
  drum,
Maryland! My Maryland!
She is not dead, nor deaf, nor
  dumb—
Huzza! she spurns the Northern
  scum!
She breathes! she burns! she'll
  come! she'll come!
Maryland! My Maryland!

Major General Benjamin F. Butler of Massachusetts

Southerners still in Washington were predicting that Confederate troops would be marching into the city by May 1. Government clerks formed a volunteer militia and drilled on the White House lawn. Winfield Scott, General in Chief of the Union army, ordered trenches dug around the Capitol and placed cannon on the bank of the Anacostia River, which flows from Maryland through Washington to the Potomac River. "The White House is turned into barracks," an aide to Lincoln wrote, adding, "A unit called the Kansas Warriors…[marches] into the East Room." Lincoln's young sons built a make-believe fort on the roof.

Baltimore's mayor and chief of police, with the approval of the governor of Maryland, had ordered the burning of the bridges that carried trains to Baltimore from Philadelphia and Harrisburg. This cut Washington off from the north. Mobs tore down poles on all telegraph lines leading to Washington. The mayor warned Lincoln in a letter "it is not possible for more soldiers to pass through Baltimore unless they fight their way at every step."

Lincoln had no way of knowing when or how—or even if—troops would reach Washington. One of his secretaries saw Lincoln late one night standing by a window and saying, "Why don't they come? Why don't they come?"

The troops who had come before the bridges went down found temporary lodging in the Capitol, the Treasury Building, and the Patent Office Building. These first arrivals, General Scott knew, were not enough to defend the city against a Confederate attack. More were needed, and they had been on the tracks now cut off from Washington.

Lincoln and Scott were awaiting soldiers under the command of Benjamin F. Butler, a wily Massachusetts politician who had been commissioned a major general. Butler's train got as far as Perryville, Maryland, on the northern bank of the Susquehanna River, where he found the ferryboat *Maryland*. He commandeered the

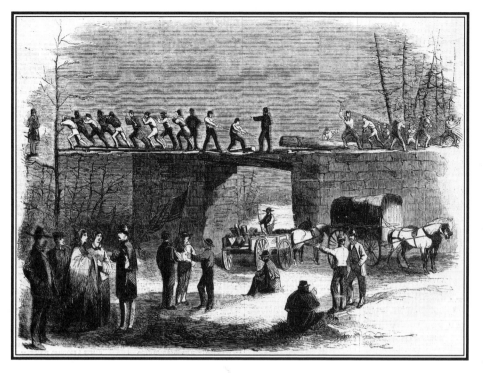

Soldiers from Major General Benjamin Butler's Eighth Massachusetts Regiment repair a railroad bridge in Annapolis that was damaged by anti-Union Marylanders.

boat and ordered the captain to take him and his men down Chesapeake Bay to Annapolis, where he knew there was a rail connection with Washington. But he soon discovered that "secesh," as Union soldiers were calling their foes, had also torn up the tracks and wrecked trains in Annapolis.

Butler pointed to a broken-down locomotive and asked if anyone could get it running. A soldier took a close look at it and said, "The engine was made in our shop. I guess I can fix her up and run her."

Butler then asked if any of the other soldiers could repair trains and lay tracks. Several stepped forward. They were former railroad men who had volunteered to carry guns to defend the Union. The men, wielding wrenches and sledgehammers, were soon re-laying rails and getting damaged cars back on track.

Yankee know-how quickly got troops to Washington, ending the crisis. Butler's triumphant arrival showed that this war needed soldiers who could fix up machinery as well as burn down bridges and cut telegraph wires. And the new President had also learned a lesson: Railroads could serve as vital supply arteries, but the arteries could be cut. And this was true for the South as well as for the North.

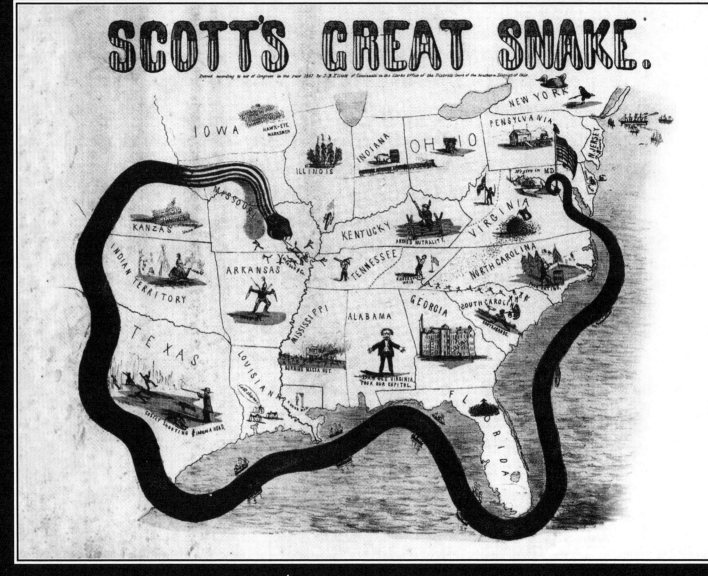

Southern states are surrounded on a map showing General in Chief Winfield Scott's plan to blockade ports along coasts and the Mississippi River. Critics labeled it the "Anaconda Plan" for the snake that kills by squeezing.

CHAPTER THREE

· THE ANACONDA PLAN ·

Both the Fort Sumter crisis and the attempt to cut off Washington showed Lincoln the importance and difficulty of handling logistics—the art and science of getting troops, weapons, and equipment where and when they are needed. He got another lesson in the same subject as he faced the challenges of assembling a large army—and a navy capable of carrying out General Scott's blockade strategy, which came to be known as the Anaconda Plan.

Just as an anaconda subdues its prey by surrounding it and then squeezing it to death, Scott's idea called for a naval blockade that, by closing Southern ports, would cut off the Confederacy from trade with the outside world. If the South were unable to sell its cotton to France or Great Britain or to import weapons or other manufactured items, it would not have the money or the supplies to fight

Winfield Scott was the Union's top general in 1861.

a war. If, at the same time, the North could close the many river ports of the Mississippi to Confederate traffic, it could divide the South and keep Texas, Arkansas, Missouri, and most of Louisiana from coming to the aid of the rest of the South.

At first the term "Anaconda Plan" was used to mock Scott's idea. Lincoln, however, supported the plan, which became part of his policy and the Union strategy for winning the war. On April 19, 1861, he issued the Proclamation of Blockade. In theory, the idea made sense, but, as Lincoln would quickly discover, the challenge of putting the plan into practice was enormous. The South had some 3,500 miles of ocean coastline, 10 major ports, 180 smaller bays, inlets, and river mouths, plus numerous coastal islands. And then there was the lower Mississippi with its endless bayous and tributaries.

Scott, who had been born in Virginia, might have seen his idea as a relatively gentle way to pressure the departing states into returning. But Lincoln soon came to understand that the naval blockade, which also called for the occupation of New Orleans and the conquest of Vicksburg, Mississippi, might better be described as a cruel necessity of the Union's war effort.

Even if only the larger ports, harbors, and cities were blocked, the plan required far more ships than the Union navy had. Lincoln's Secretary of the Navy, Gideon Welles, discovered that the Union had only 90 ships. Of these, 48 were laid up and out of commission and 30 more were on duty all over the world, many months from home waters. Welles had only a dozen ships available for blockade duty, and half of those were obsolete sailing ships. Only 5 or 6 modern steamships were available. The Union needed more ships, and fast.

Welles summoned home nearly all the ships on foreign duty. He ordered the building of 8 sloops (small

Gideon Welles built an iron-clad Union navy.

ships with a single mast), 23 gunboats, and 12 paddlewheel steamers designed for river operations. He also started buying civilian ships that could be converted for naval duty. By June, Welles had managed to assign 36 ships to blockade duty, and he continued to add more. But even if the Union put all the shipyards in the North to work, it would take time to build enough ships for a fully effective blockade.

On April 3, 1861, Abraham Lincoln attended the wedding celebration of Nannie Buchanan, daughter of Captain Franklin Buchanan, commandant of the Washington Navy Yard and a Marylander who sympathized with the South. If the President had hoped the gesture would charm his host into remaining with the Union, he failed. Within three weeks, Buchanan, who incorrectly expected that Maryland was about to secede from the Union, went over to the Confederacy. But Lincoln's attendance at the wedding would pay off in unexpected ways. It was at that event that Lincoln was introduced to Commander John A. Dahlgren, who would

A ship for the Union blockade fleet begins to take shape at the New York Naval Shipyard, which was also unofficially known as the Brooklyn Navy Yard.

soon succeed to Captain Buchanan's job.

Virginia took the first steps toward leaving the Union in late April, though the decision would not be official or final for about a month. If Maryland had made the same choice, the capital of the United States would have been surrounded by enemy territory.

At the same time, not only states but also people began leaving the Union. Captain Buchanan, Colonel Robert E. Lee, Major Thomas Jackson (soon to become famous as "Stonewall" Jackson), Brigadier General Joseph Johnston, Commander Matthew Fontaine Maury, and a host of others switched their allegiance to the Southern cause, taking with them their skills, experience, and detailed knowledge about how the Union government and its armed forces worked.

Welles also knew that the Southerners would seize whatever Union naval facilities they could. The giant Gosport Navy Yard (today known as the Norfolk Navy Yard) in Virginia, near the mouth of Chesapeake Bay, was especially vulnerable.

As more and more people left Washington to serve the Confederacy, Commander Dahlgren discovered that he had only about 150 workers at the Navy Yard to help him prepare to withstand the siege or invasion that was predicted to come at any time. He armed and fitted river steamers, laid in supplies, and secured his ordnance (military weaponry) and stocks of gunpowder.

· MILITARY MASS PRODUCTION ·

John Dahlgren, a naval officer who was also an energetic inventor and engineer, started work at the Navy Yard in 1847 with the assignment of building artillery rockets. His innovative designs included a naval bayonet, a naval howitzer, and a cannon that became known as the Dahlgren gun. It remained the standard armament for U.S. Navy ships long after the Civil War. Dahlgren understood that for a weapon to be useful it needed more than a good design. It had to be manufactured in large enough quantities to be effective, which meant all of the parts needed to assemble it also had to be mass-produced.

U.S. Government armories at Springfield, Massachusetts, and Harpers Ferry, Virginia, had developed techniques and machines for producing interchangeable parts that allowed for rapid assembly of the product and for rapid replacement of broken or damaged parts. In one pre-war demonstration, ten randomly selected rifles built in ten different years were taken apart. A worker was able to assemble ten working muskets using the mixed-and-matched parts. The mass production of interchangeable parts spread from the armories to civilian factories, nearly all of which were in the North. The result was improved productivity and output for all types of military supplies once the war came.

John Dahlgren poses with a 50-pounder Dahlgren gun.

Dahlgren installed gaslights at the Navy Yard, allowing work to go on day and night, even on Sundays. The yard was alive with the kind of technical innovation and modern mass production found in the North. In the yard were heavy steam hammers for forming boat anchors, a laboratory for developing gunpowder, and a chain-cable shop. The yard also had a rolling mill for shaping metal, brass and iron foundries for manufacturing cannon, and specialized steam-driven machinery for making rifled artillery pieces and mortars, along with cannon shells by the hundreds and percussion caps and rifle balls by the tens of thousands daily.

Under Dahlgren, the Washington Navy Yard was a center for armament technology. And Lincoln would be there to see it. Throughout the war, Lincoln was a frequent visitor to the Navy Yard, examining new weapons, seeing and hearing them being tested and demonstrated.

The Confederates were even less prepared for war than the Union. The North had a government, a treasury, an army, and a navy. The one-time Union naval officers who went over to the Confederacy faced a task far more

Flames roar through the Union's Gosport Navy Yard in Norfolk.
It was deliberately set afire to keep its ships from being used by the Confederates.

daunting than the one that faced Lincoln and Welles. As one former Confederate naval officer put it after the war, "until the organization of the Confederate States, there was not one ship owned by any State, nor the least effort made to procure one;...there was not a piece of ordnance of any kind; nor a yard in which a yawl-boat could be built; not a machine-shop capable, without material alteration, of constructing the simplest piece of naval machinery; not a rope-yard, not a percussion-cap machine, only one powder mill, no supply of nitre, or sulphur, or lead—not the least preparation of any kind."

Huge as the North's technological and industrial advantages may have been, the events of April 19 and 20, 1861, in Norfolk, Virginia, were disastrous for the Union navy—and a gift beyond price for the Confederate navy.

Rightly assuming that the Gosport Navy Yard was about to be seized by secessionists, the Union navy evacuated the yard, burning and deliberately sinking the ships there to keep them out of Southern hands. Thanks to a whole series of mistakes, including failures to follow orders, resistance from local residents, and just plain bad luck, not everything in the yard was destroyed.

The Union forces left behind nearly 2,000 naval guns as well as workshops, a dry dock (a special dock where water can be pumped out so that a ship in it can be more easily repaired), and supplies for shipbuilding. The Confederates moved in and took over, even managing to raise and repair several of the sunken ships, including the U.S.S. *Merrimack*. The failure to destroy that ship would have huge consequences.

President Lincoln, once a rail-splitter, swings a maul to fight the dragon of rebellion, but the Constitution limits his power. "TamOny Hall" refers to corrupt Tammany Hall politicians in New York City.

CHAPTER FOUR

·LEARNING WAR·

In the spring of 1861, Lincoln could stand in the White House, look through his telescope, and see a Confederate flag flying above the roof of Marshall House, an inn across the Potomac River in Alexandria, Virginia. He knew that if he did not act, Confederate soldiers would rally to that flag. Washington could well come under fire from cannon on the heights directly across the river, and the White House itself was in range of artillery weapons.

Since his election, Lincoln had already learned plenty of hard lessons about how—and how not—to deal with a crisis. He had faced the threat of Washington being cut off from the North and the danger to the capital from Confederate sympathizers who remained in the city. Now he had to confront the threat of attack from the South: Virginia was about to become enemy territory.

What Lincoln saw through his telescope

Lincoln knew that he would have to push the Confederate forces back so that Washington was out of artillery range. But he had to judge the politics of the situation as well. He believed that he could not invade Virginia because the state was technically still in the Union. In April and early May, the state went through a long and complicated process of proclamations and of legislative and popular votes that, step by step, took Virginia out of the Union, recognized the Confederacy, and paved the way for Virginia to join that new nation. Then, on May 23, 1861, in a move expected for weeks, Virginians overwhelmingly voted to enter the Confederacy.

Lincoln moved quickly. The next day in predawn darkness, Union soldiers—on Lincoln's orders—crossed the Potomac and occupied Virginia soil. President Lincoln had truly become Commander in Chief.

Most Union troops crossed bridges that linked Washington with Virginia. Almost directly across the river was Arlington House, the vacant home of Robert E. Lee and his family, which immediately became a headquarters for Union forces. (The mansion still stands, and its grounds are now Arlington National Cemetery.) Another force crossed the river in steamboats that sailed from the Navy Yard and tied up at wharves in Alexandria. No resistance was met by the forces who crossed the bridges or by those who entered Alexandria. The few Southern volunteers defending the town had retreated as soon as the invasion began, so there was no battle. But blood was shed.

Colonel Elmer Ellsworth, leader of a New York infantry regiment, spotted the Confederate flag flying from the rooftop of Marshall House. He rushed in, ran up the stairs, went to the roof, and ripped down the flag. As he descended the stairs, James W. Jackson, the innkeeper, fatally shot him.

Ellsworth's death personally touched the President. Twenty-four-year-old Ellsworth, a close friend of Lincoln and his family, had been one of the soldiers living in the White House, where he had played with the Lincoln children. The President burst into tears when he heard about Ellsworth's death. When he saw his body, Lincoln exclaimed, "My boy! My boy! Was it necessary this sacrifice should be?" That his decision had caused the death of his friend affected Lincoln deeply.

Lincoln's order to occupy Alexandria defied the strategy of General Scott, a Virginian who was against invading the South. He believed that the so-called Anaconda Plan (although he had come up with the plan, he didn't like the name) "could bring them to terms with less bloodshed than by any other plan."

General Scott's view of the war was so different from Lincoln's that Lincoln felt he had to overrule him. The United States Constitution states, "The President shall be Commander in Chief of the Army and Navy of the United States, and of the Militia of the several States, when called into the actual Service of the United States." However, no President had ever fully assumed that role. Distance and bad communication had made that impossible. But Lincoln had the telegraph and the railroad.

Colonel Elmer Ellsworth clutches his chest, fatally shot by a secessionist innkeeper. Moments later, Union soldiers killed the shooter.

And the war was—almost literally—in his own front yard.

He believed, as he told a trusted military adviser, that he had to take "these army matters" into his own hands.

He set about educating himself. To learn more about war, he would borrow books on military strategy from the Library of Congress.

But the war would not wait for him to complete his studies. Following through on the invasion, Union army engineers immediately began building forts in Virginia to protect the Potomac bridges. In a few frantic weeks, soldiers dug foundations for forts, took possession of land needed for defenses, and wiped out a forest on Arlington Heights. Squads of soldiers felled rows of trees so that their sharpened branches faced outward and downward in a 19th-century version of barbed wire.

Most of the people in Alexandria fled. Union officers took over mansions, public buildings, and even churches. The city became the headquarters for the U.S. Military Railroad and the site of one of the Union's largest hospitals.

Lincoln acted to protect against other threats to the capital city. He claimed special constitutional powers to suspend the writ of habeas corpus. Acting under that authority, Union soldiers put Baltimore's chief of police and mayor in jail, along with 31 members of Maryland's state legislature. They all spent two months behind bars.

The invasion of Virginia protected Washington from cannon fire but not from an attack by the Confederate army. Lincoln realized that it was only a matter of time before the Confederates would assemble enough men to move against the city. He wanted to strike first.

Lincoln knew he would need the telegraph to keep in touch with his troops as they moved into Virginia. When Lincoln arrived in Washington, the War Department did not even have its own telegraph connection. To send a message, the War Department sent a man to the central telegraph office. If there was a line, he stood in it. At the counter, he handed a paper to a clerk, who handed it to a telegrapher, who put it in the stack of outgoing messages to wait its turn.

Soon after Lincoln took the oath of office, he gave orders to have a telegraph line strung directly to the War Department Building, which was a short distance from the White House. He quickly formed a habit that he maintained throughout his presidency. During the war, by day and by night, President Lincoln walked to the War

· HABEAS CORPUS ·

President Lincoln, a skilled courtroom lawyer who had studied the law carefully, was determined not to let Washington be cut off from the North again. He turned to Article I, Section 9 of the U. S. Constitution: "The privilege of the Writ of Habeas Corpus shall not be suspended, unless when in Cases of Rebellion or Invasion the public Safety may require it."

Habeas corpus is part of a Latin phrase—*habeas corpus ad subjiciendum*—meaning that a person cannot be detained without having the charges reviewed by a judge who, after examining the evidence, rules if the person should be held for trial or released. In other words, it guarantees that a person cannot be thrown into jail without just cause.

Lincoln used his power to proclaim a special status for rail and telegraph lines between the capital and Philadelphia and suspended habeas corpus along that stretch of America. Authorized to arrest anyone suspected of acting against—or just speaking against—the Union, soldiers began rounding up Southern sympathizers in the region.

Lincoln believed that he had to suspend habeas corpus "or surrender the existence of the Government." He believed that if the Commander in Chief was not allowed to arrest spies and military saboteurs, there soon wouldn't be anything left for him to command.

In February 1862, judging that the Maryland threat had eased, Lincoln restored the right of habeas corpus, but he periodically suspended it at other times in other places when he felt it was necessary for the military to enforce the law. Later in the war, Lincoln denied the right to all "prisoners of war, spies, or aiders and abettors of the enemy."

President Lincoln sits at a desk in the War Department's busy telegraph office, ready to send and receive messages about the war.

Department, accompanied by one or more bodyguards. There, in the telegraph office, he ran the war by Morse code, writing and reading messages. Hardly a day passed without a presidential visit to that office.

While Commander in Chief Lincoln was learning his job, General Scott continued to wage war the same way he had during the Mexican War two decades before. In 1847 he had led the U.S. forces that conquered Mexico. Scott had run that war the way generals had always run wars: From their headquarters behind the lines, they sent out couriers who carried orders to fighting units at the front. Soldiers then carried out these orders by responding to bugles and drums or shouted commands.

Scott had been born in 1786 into a nation whose goods moved on rutted, muddy roads that were so bad that they couldn't be relied on for heavy cargo. He was bound by his own experience and his knowledge of how to supply armies by shipping goods over water. He had no appreciation for the railroad and the telegraph as tools of war.

Even as his chief general clung to the old ways, President Lincoln came to understand the army's officers were as new at war as the young men who had been answering his call for volunteers—and they were very new indeed. The generals told Lincoln not to send his soldiers into battle quite yet. They are green, the generals said. Lincoln, at a council of war, shook his head and said to one of the generals, "You are green, it is true, but they [the Confederate soldiers] are green, also; you are all green alike."

Finally, under Lincoln's prodding, the army machinery began to creak into motion, inspired as much by the calendar as by the Confederates. Many of the 35,000

Union soldiers posted in Arlington were close to the end of their three-month enlistments and could leave the army as soon as their 90-day hitch ended.

The Confederates had 22,000 men at Manassas, a railroad junction about 30 miles southwest of Washington. Another 12,000 Confederates, under Brigadier General Joseph E. Johnston, held the Shenandoah Valley at Winchester, some 30 miles down the railroad line from Harpers Ferry, Virginia. On July 16, 1861, under Major General Irvin McDowell, a Union army of about 28,500 marched off toward Manassas on what was called a campaign to take Richmond, the Rebel capital. In ragged columns the Union troops jammed dusty country roads. Some were in colorful Zouave uniforms. The Garibaldi Guards wore green-plumed hats. Soldiers, many of them teenagers, wandered out of the line of march to pick blackberries. It took the army two and a half days to cover the 20 miles to the hamlet of Centreville on the road to Manassas, about three miles northeast of a creek called Bull Run.

As McDowell's scouts probed the size and locations of the Confederate forces, his Southern opponent, Major General Pierre G. T. Beauregard, turned to modern technology: He telegraphed Johnston, ordering him to march his men from Winchester to the nearest railroad track and head for Manassas. Beauregard also benefited from espionage, learning about at least part of McDowell's plan through a spy. Mrs. Rose O'Neale Greenhow, a beautiful and popular Washington hostess, had friends in high places. She got the information to Beauregard with the aid of a charming Southern woman who was allowed to pass through Union lines.

On July 20, as McDowell called a council of war to outline his attack plan for the next day, officers told him that they had been hearing trains chugging in and out of Manassas all day. That surely meant that Beauregard was getting reinforcements. But McDowell would not change his plan. At 2 a.m. on Sunday, July 21, he launched his complex attack, which required a series of maneuvers that would have been challenging enough for seasoned troops, let alone 90-day militia men. He sent two thrusts toward the Confederate line while his main force of about 13,000 men headed north to a ford. The Confederates saw through

· WEST POINT ·

Nearly every general on both sides, and many of the lower-ranking officers North and South, were graduates of the U.S. Military Academy at West Point. In 55 of the 60 largest battles of the Civil War there were West Point graduates in command on both sides. The other 5 had a West Pointer in charge on just one side. Most of the men who became senior commanders in the Civil War had also fought in the Mexican-American War.

One result of all this was that, to a degree rare in history, many of the commanders on both sides knew their enemies. They had gone to West Point with them, fought alongside them, and worked with them. It also meant that nearly all Confederate officers had detailed knowledge of how the opposing army worked because they had

Ulysses S. Grant
West Point Class of 1843

Robert E. Lee
West Point Class of 1829

all served in it before the war.

All West Pointers learned the tactics of Napoleon from the works of Antoine Henri Jomini, a Swiss officer who had served with Napoleon. Two graduates—Henry W. Halleck (who later served for two years, without particular distinction, as Lincoln's General in Chief) and Dennis Hart Mahan—wrote books on strategy and tactics that were in large part based on Jomini, and their books were taught at West Point. In the Mexican-American War, West Point graduates (including Grant and Lee), put those tactics to

work and won battle after battle as well as the war itself. But those tactics were written before the railroad, the telegraph, and the long-range rifle changed the way armies moved, communicated, and fought.

Jomini's strategic ideas were just as important as his tactics. Among many other assumptions in his work was the idea that wars should be fought not only for limited objectives but also by professional soldiers, with little or no thought of what the civilian government or the people wanted. He also believed the civilian population should be left alone as much as possible.

Although both the North and the South started out trying to fight the war that way, both sides found out the hard way that many of Jomini's theories weren't going to apply to the American Civil War.

the diversion plan and, from signal stations on hilltops, passed a warning by wigwag, a flag communications system invented by a federal army officer but used this day by a pupil, Edward Porter Alexander, an army officer who had gone South.

When the battle began, the War Department's military telegraph line was strung on a bridge crossing the Potomac River and into Virginia as far as the village of Fairfax Court House, near Alexandria. From there, couriers on horseback carried messages to and from McDowell's headquarters. A telegrapher, Andrew Carnegie (later to become one of the nation's wealthiest industrialists and philanthropists), had set up this Union army version of a short-distance Pony Express.

Lincoln, members of his Cabinet, General Scott, and other officers gathered in the telegraph office at the War Department to follow the battle through the messages coming in from Manassas. Believing that he could do

Wigwag signals were sent from hilltops or towers.

nothing to affect the outcome of the battle, the aging Scott soon went off to take a nap.

Throughout the morning and into the afternoon, Lincoln read encouraging telegrams from McDowell. In the afternoon, the dispatches from the battle stopped coming. Lincoln and the others sensed that something had gone wrong. Then, suddenly, the *click-click-click* of the telegraph began again, tapping out a single sentence: OUR ARMY IS RETREATING. Another, from a captain in the ranks who had managed to get to a telegraph courier, read: THE DAY IS LOST. SAVE WASHINGTON AND THE REMNANTS OF THIS ARMY....

Occasionally, unofficial and technical messages went out from the War Department to the telegraph operators in Virginia. One of them, 16-year-old Charles Jaques, sent an urgent—and personal—message telling Washington that more and more soldiers were passing his station as they retreated in a panic toward Washington. Jaques said he was going to join them. Back came

Union horses and men rapidly rush to Washington in the panicky retreat from Bull Run (Manassas), first battle of the Civil War.

a private message: WAR DEPARTMENT, WASHINGTON, TO JAQUES, OPERATOR, SPRINGFIELD. IF YOU KEEP YOUR OFFICE OPEN UNTIL YOU HAVE PERMISSION TO CLOSE IT, YOU WILL BE REWARDED. IF YOU CLOSE IT WITHOUT SUCH PERMISSION, YOU WILL BE SHOT.

Joining in the retreat were members of Congress and prominent men and women of Washington who had taken picnic lunches in their carriages and ridden out to see the battle. Fleeing civilians collided with fleeing soldiers. Drivers of horse-drawn ambulances loaded with wounded cut away horses, mounted them, and rode off, abandoning the casualties in their charge. A Senator who had lost his carriage climbed onto a stray army mule. It was anything but an orderly retreat. It was a disaster.

Through the night and into the next day, while others in the North were wallowing in panic and despair, Lincoln took up a pen and began writing, jotting down ideas—"Let the volunteer forces…be constantly drilled, disciplined, and instructed….Let the three month forces, who decline to enter the longer service, be discharged as rapidly as circumstances will permit…."

He was the Commander in Chief, working on the strategy of what he now knew would be a long war.

Even before the shambles of the First Battle of Bull Run (or the First Battle of Manassas as it was known to the Confederates), Lincoln had been open to any ideas and innovations that might serve the cause—even if they came from out of the bright blue sky itself.

A summer 1861 balloon's-eye view of the Capitol, with the new dome under construction. Lowe sent his

CHAPTER FIVE

· RIDING THE WINDS OF BATTLE ·

On June 18, 1861, a strange shape loomed in the Washington sky. It was a giant lighter-than-air balloon named *Enterprise*. Aboard was the balloon's 28-year-old maker, the grandly named Thaddeus Sobieski Constantine Lowe. A telegraph cable ran from the balloon to the ground and connected to the War Department. While aloft, Lowe sent this telegram to the President:

SIR: THIS POINT OF OBSERVATION COMMANDS AN AREA NEARLY 50 MILES IN DIAMETER. THE CITY, WITH ITS GIRDLE OF ENCAMPMENTS, PRESENTS A SUPERB SCENE. I HAVE PLEASURE IN SENDING YOU THIS FIRST DISPATCH EVER TELEGRAPHED FROM AN AERIAL STATION, AND IN ACKNOWLEDGING INDEBTEDNESS FOR YOUR ENCOURAGEMENT FOR THE OPPORTUNITY OF DEMONSTRATING THE AVAILABILITY OF THE SCIENCE OF AERONAUTICS IN THE MILITARY SERVICE OF THE COUNTRY.

Professor Thaddeus Lowe, Union aeronaut

After Lowe sent his aerial telegram, his balloon was towed to White House grounds, where it floated overhead while Lowe was President Lincoln's overnight guest. The President saw to it that the aeronaut's ideas were listened to, in spite of the objections of traditionalists in the War Department.

No fewer than three attempts were made to get a balloon into position for the First Battle of Bull Run on July 21, 1861, including attempts by Lowe's rival aeronauts. One balloon ran into a telegraph pole and burst. Another, towed toward the battle by a horse-drawn carriage, became wedged in a tree and tore open. Lowe's own balloon was caught up in the general retreat and never even reached the battlefield.

After the battle, rumors swept Washington that the Confederates were going to march on from Manassas and invade the capital. Lowe decided to find out for himself.

On July 24, he made a free ascent—in other words, he went up without any tether connecting him to the ground or any means of keeping his balloon in a fixed position. His balloon lofted him three miles high. He could see that the main body of Confederate troops was still near Manassas. After being fired upon by nervous Northern troops, he landed outside the Union lines. Both he and his balloon were rescued, and he was able to report his observations the next day, helping to tamp down the near-panic in Washington.

Observation balloons thus quickly demonstrated both their promise and their drawbacks. They could provide a superb view of the enemy, but they were unwieldy and awkward to transport and were unreliable and difficult—or even impossible—to control once they were in the air. From the perspective of the 21st century, the benefit of being able to see, directly, where the enemy is and what he is doing seems utterly plain and to outweigh the drawbacks. But 19th-century military men were suspicious of the strange new gimmickry, and—to them at least—the aeronauts seemed every bit as eccentric and

unmilitary as their gaudy balloons. But Lincoln, at least, could see the potential.

Lincoln wrote to General Scott urging him to listen to Lowe. When Scott declined four separate times to meet with the aeronaut, Lowe returned to the President's office to protest. Lincoln heard him out, stood up, put on his stovepipe hat, personally escorted the balloonist into the general's office, and got Scott's attention that way.

Granted official support, Lowe and his rival Union aeronauts were able to work on technical problems, nearly all of which involved the simple physics of how a balloon generated lift.

But the aeronauts had other battles to fight. "My troubles had barely begun," wrote Lowe, "so cumbersome was the official machinery, so interwoven the red tape."

Another Union aeronaut, John La Mountain, was invited to demonstrate aerial observation by Major General Benjamin Butler, commander of Fortress Monroe at Hampton Roads, in Virginia. Since the Confederates had taken control of Gosport Navy Yard in April, Monroe was the only Union stronghold at the

· LIFTING GAS ·

The lighter-than-air balloon works on a simple principle: Fill it with a gas that has lower density than the air outside. The balloon will be buoyant because the combined weight of the balloon and the gas in it will be less than the weight of the air that would otherwise occupy that space. If the vehicle attached to it is light enough, then the balloon will float upward.

One way to make a balloon lighter than air is to fill it with normal air that has been heated. Heat causes air to expand—in other words to become less dense. Make a large enough volume of air hot enough, and the difference in density will produce significant lift. But a hot-air balloon must either land when the air in it gets cold or carry along a heat source. In the Civil War era that would have meant carrying an open fire and the

Lowe, raising his hand near the gasbag, supervises the use of his hydrogen generators to fill a balloon far from city limits.

fuel for it up into the air in the balloon's gondola, or basket. That would add weight and risk a disastrous fire, so the heat source was left on the ground. For that reason a hot-air balloon couldn't stay aloft very long.

The other solution was even simpler—just fill the balloon with a gas that is naturally less dense than air, even at normal temperatures. Town gas was the gas used to light public spaces and homes—hence the term "gaslight." Town gas was usually extracted from coal. That kind of gas contained methane, carbon monoxide, hydrogen, and various other combustible substances. It was less dense and, therefore, lighter than air.

All aeronauts had to do was hook up their balloons to the town gas pipes and fill them up. But if an aeronaut wanted to lift off from somewhere outside the city, he would have to fill up his balloon using the city gas line and then tow the huge and very unwieldy gasbag to the launch site.

Lowe and his rivals soon learned that, in wartime, they had to transport balloons *before* inflating them. But how to transport the gas needed to inflate the balloon? The answer was to use hydrogen. Lowe invented a portable hydrogen generator based on a well-known chemical process: When sulphuric acid is mixed with iron, the resulting reaction releases hydrogen gas. His generators could be transported on boats or pulled by horses—a simple, reliable system that would generate hydrogen in the field.

entrance to Chesapeake Bay. La Mountain made several flights to observe Confederate activity in the vicinity of the York and James Rivers and their nearby facilities.

That same month, the Union navy purchased the *George Washington Parke Custis*, a coal barge, named for the first President's step-grandson—who also happened to be Robert E. Lee's father-in-law. At the Washington Navy Yard, under the supervision of Captain Dahlgren, she was modified by installing a large, flat deck and one of Lowe's hydrogen generators. On November 11, 1861, the *G.W.P. Custis* served as the launching platform for a balloon that would observe Confederate activity on the Virginia side of the Potomac River, near Mattawoman Creek. These ascents marked the beginnings of naval aviation. The modifications to the *G.W.P. Custis* stake her claim to be the world's first aircraft carrier designed for the purpose.

The aeronauts scored other achievements. La Mountain made nighttime flights to count Rebel campfires in order to estimate troop numbers. Major General Butler himself went aloft several times. On September 24, 1861, Lowe became the first man in history to direct

Lowe's balloon Washington *lifts off from the G.W.P. Custis. This mobile base allowed wide-ranging operations.*

artillery fire from the air, communicating via a telegraph line that ran from the balloon's gondola directly to the gunnery crew three miles away.

Aside from their other drawbacks, balloons cannot be steered or guided. If a balloon is not tethered to the ground, it is at the mercy of wind and weather. But even if an aeronaut could not steer or aim a balloon, he could change his direction of flight by going higher or lower to catch winds that blow in different directions at different altitudes. He could lower the craft by releasing gas from the balloon or go higher by dropping extra weight, called ballast. La Mountain made several free ascents from Union-held areas by riding low-altitude winds westward toward Rebel-held areas and then dropping ballast so he could fly higher and catch a ride home on upper-level eastbound winds.

Coming in for a landing after a free ascent was always risky. The aeronaut could be forced to make a crash landing, be blown off course, get caught in trees, or even be shot at—sometimes by his own troops. More than once, Union soldiers fired at Union balloonists they believed were working for the other side.

For all of the technical improvements in airborne observation from the summer of 1861 to the spring of 1862, there was not that much for aeronauts to observe. They could see where the other side's troops were, but neither side's troops were doing much fighting. Winter weather from about November on was part of the problem. Armies simply could not march to battle over the dirt—and mud—roads of 1860s America in the winter. A road that would bear up under occasional farm traffic would be churned into a muddy, icy, glue-like mess if an army of thousands of men, carts, and horses moved over it. Snow, ice, rain, and cold essentially shut down the war for winter every year. But the biggest cause of delay was not Mother Nature but human nature—especially in the form of Major General George B. McClellan.

Only a month or two before Bull Run, both sides had confidently expected a short war. But the results of that battle were not what anyone expected. The defeated Billy Yank did not give up, and the victorious Johnny Reb didn't march on Washington.

Both sides slowly started to realize that it was going to

· GUNNING FOR THE BALLOONS ·

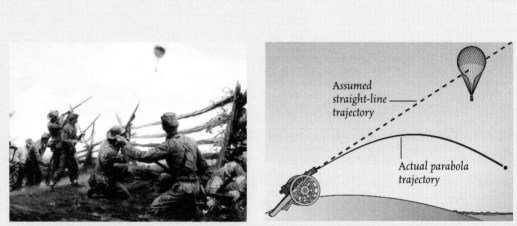

Assumed straight-line trajectory

Actual parabola trajectory

Rebel soldiers never hit any Union balloons—thanks to the laws of ballistics, illustrated above.

A giant gasbag hanging motionless in midair would seem like a tempting and easy target—especially if it's filled with a flammable gas! Yet no Civil War observation balloon was ever shot down. How did the aeronauts stay in the air?

First off, the balloons were simply out of range. They were raised from a position well behind the lines and hung hundreds or thousands of feet up in the air. Rifles just couldn't shoot that far or that high. Cannon had the range—but a projectile fired up from a cannon or rifle must travel in a rising and falling curve called a parabola. An artilleryman aiming at a balloon would have to compute the exact distance to the balloon and its precise altitude, and then figure out a shooting angle that would cause the curved flight path of the cannon-ball to intercept the balloon. Artillery men didn't deal with such complicated math. They were trained to hit a general area, note the impact point, and adjust their fire to zero in on the intended target after two or three shots. Besides, Civil War cannon were designed to strike targets on the ground. They couldn't be raised, or elevated, enough for a shot at a balloon.

None of that stopped the men on the ground from trying. The Confederate troops hated the aloof, airborne spy balloons. Whenever they saw a balloon, they didn't stop to bother with ballistics math. They simply opened fire on it with every rifle and cannon they had, hoping that the gasbag would sail into a wall of fire. There were close calls, but no balloons were hit. The Confederates concentrated their fire as the balloon was just taking off or landing, hoping it would be an easier target when closer to the ground. Sometimes they aimed, not for the balloon, but for the ground crew and support equipment at the launch site. As much as by luck as anything else, these attacks did very little harm.

This cartoon pokes fun at the "masterly inactivity" of McClellan and Confederate Major General Beauregard during the winter of 1861–62.

be a longer and more complex war than they had expected—and both sides realized that they had done next to nothing to prepare for it. The Union and Confederate forces almost seemed to draw back, to pause before plunging deeper into the strange and forbidding sea of unknowns that was the war. There were skirmishes and brisk fights here and there, and important seizures and captures—including the Union victory in New Orleans—but no engagements on the scale of First Bull Run between August 1861 and early 1862.

Shortly after First Bull Run, Lincoln decided what the Union Army of the Potomac needed was a skillful organizer, so he brought in McClellan, a veteran of the Mexican War and chief engineer and vice president of the Illinois Central Railroad. McClellan promptly set to work getting his men properly fed, sheltered, equipped, and clothed.

He took the defeated, disorganized, and dispirited troops around the capital city and turned them into a powerful military machine. But the general seemed very reluctant to put that machine to any real use.

Month after month went by, with Lincoln urging the army into battle and McClellan insisting the men needed more training, more equipment, more time. Lincoln, getting more and more frustrated, at one point said, "If McClellan is not using the army, I should like to borrow it for a while."

Not wishing to repeat the disaster at Bull Run, McClellan developed an elaborate plan that used an amphibious landing. Rather than march his army overland, he would use ships to take them to a landing point 60 miles southeast of Richmond.

The plan took advantage of the Union's strength at sea.

The North's ability to transport soldiers and equipment by water didn't guarantee victory. Here, a mighty Union fleet moves McClellan's troops as they retreat down the Virginia Peninsula.

The Confederates would not be able to stop waterborne troop movements. McClellan would sail his troops down the Potomac River to Chesapeake Bay, then land on the Virginia Peninsula, a thumb-shaped piece of land that separates the York and James Rivers. Fortress Monroe, solidly in Union control, stood at the tip of the peninsula. McClellan planned to march on the Southern capital before the main body of the Confederate army, in camp just south of Washington, could get into position to oppose his army.

McClellan kept his plans secret until they were well advanced. It was not until February 1862 that McClellan was finally pressured into detailing his plans to the President.

Lincoln, who favored a direct overland assault on the Confederate army at Manassas, had his doubts. He wrote to McClellan asking five pointed questions: "Does not your plan involve a greatly larger expenditure of time and money than mine? Wherein is a victory more certain by your plan than mine? Wherein is a victory more valuable by your plan than mine? In fact would it not be less valuable in this that it would break no great line of the enemy's communication while mine would? [A direct attack might cut off the enemy's line of retreat to home territory, but McClellan's amphibious attack could not do that.] In case of disaster would not a safe retreat be more difficult by your plan than by mine?" McClellan replied at length, and Lincoln, not altogether convinced, reluctantly deferred to the military professional and accepted McClellan's plan with some modifications.

McClellan had another vital area of disagreement with President Lincoln. Lincoln, the supposed military amateur, continually urged McClellan to go after the Confederate army. McClellan, on the other hand, seemed convinced that the capture of Richmond would all but end the war.

The loss of Richmond would certainly have dealt a serious blow to the Southerners, but it would not have beaten them. When the end of the war finally came in 1865, it was the defeat of armies, not the capture of cities, that doomed the Confederacy. But McClellan could not or would not see this.

As the campaign finally got underway in March of 1862, Lowe and his fellow balloonists, operating off the *Custis* in Chesapeake Bay and on the James River as well as from bases on land, made numerous ascensions. The aeronauts observed Confederate forces so clearly that they could almost count the soldiers, one by one. They could estimate the size of units by counting their campfires at night or by noting how large a cloud of dust was raised by a maneuvering unit. They produced remarkably detailed reports and drawings of the enemy positions. But, like so many other military commanders before and since, McClellan seemed to prefer woefully inaccurate military intelligence that confirmed what he already believed: that he was outnumbered 2 to 1. In fact, the Army of the Potomac, at more than 120,000 men, was nearly twice the size of the roughly 65,000 Confederate forces in the area—only 13,000 of whom were in position to confront the enemy in the early phases of the operation.

Lowe detected the Confederate evacuation of Yorktown just before a planned Union attack on what were suddenly empty fortifications. McClellan steadily advanced, forcing the Rebels to retreat again and again, until Union troops were close enough to hear the hours being struck in the bell towers of Richmond. On May 31, Lowe spotted Brigadier General Johnston's forces moving forward to attack. The aerial scout descended and rode a horse six miles to warn McClellan. A Union officer stated that "[i]t may be safely claimed that the Union Army was saved from destruction at the Battle of Fair Oaks [Virginia]…by the frequent and accurate reports of Professor Lowe."

On June 1, just as McClellan seemed to be nearing victory, Johnston was wounded in the second day of the Battle of Fair Oaks. Confederate President Jefferson Davis appointed a new commander of the Army of Northern Virginia: General Robert E. Lee.

Lee concentrated his smaller forces against isolated parts of the larger Union forces. In a series of battles known as the Seven Days, Lee used every tactic and strategic maneuver he knew to trick McClellan into thinking he faced a larger force. McClellan, always ready to believe the enemy was more numerous, chose to disregard the information he was getting from the aeronauts as to the size and disposition of Lee's troops. He decided to fall back from his position in front of Richmond. The Peninsular Campaign ended with retreat and evacuation, with the Union forces stopping only when they were

· LAND TORPEDOES ·

As Rebel troops were retreating toward Richmond during the Peninsular Campaign, they covered their retreat by laying the first land-torpedo fields (what we would call mine fields) of the war. Men in the rearguard buried 8- and 10-inch artillery shells a few inches underground in the paths of pursuing Union soldiers. Each shell had a fuse designed to detonate (blow up) the shell when it struck a target. Southern troops were quick to realize that the shell would also explode if struck by the foot of a Union soldier or the hoof of a Union horse. The exploding shells killed, wounded, and—most of all—panicked Union soldiers, who were stunned by these invisible new weapons.

Another type of torpedo was controlled by a hidden soldier who could set it off by pulling a cord. After Northern troops pulled back from the Southern capital, the Rebels buried hundreds of mines along approaches to the city.

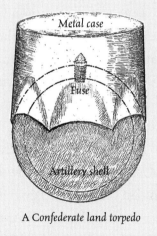

A Confederate land torpedo

protected by the guns of Fortress Monroe and the navy.

One half-forgotten success of the Peninsular Campaign was that it demonstrated the vast potential of amphibious operations and, more generally, of combined army-navy operations. By maintaining and continuously strengthening the blockade, by delivering troops and supplies over water, by denying the Confederates the chance to use water-borne transport, by bombarding targets from the sea while the army attacked by land, the navy greatly strengthened the army's hand. In modern terms, the navy's operations would be called a force amplifier. One Southern historian of the Confederate navy argued that many Union army victories could be traced back to support from the Union navy and even went so far as to argue that, without naval support, the Union army would have lost the war.

After the Peninsular Campaign, the Unions' use of balloons all but ended. There were a few half-hearted Union ballooning attempts in early 1863, but they came to nothing.

The Confederates also tried to use observation balloons during the Peninsular Campaign. But they had far fewer resources than the Northerners—and they seemed to have much worse luck.

After the war, former Confederate officer Edwin Porter Alexander wrote: "I have never understood why the enemy abandoned the use of military balloons early in 1863 after having used them extensively up to that time. Even if the observers never saw anything, they would have been worth all they cost for the annoyance and delays they caused us in trying to keep our movements out of their sight."

The most important reason that the Union army abandoned balloons was also the simplest: The commanders—such as McClellan—who made use of this new-fangled gadgetry of gas generators, ropes, and brightly colored balloons were discredited. The plain fact was that those who had made observation balloons part of their operations had not won battles.

But at almost the same time as McClellan's Peninsular Campaign was leaving Washington, another technological revolution in warfare broke out—a revolution based, not on fragile gasbags in the air, but on heavy iron on the water.

The Union's Monitor *moves in on the* C.S.S. *Virginia. Prior to battle, the Monitor's crew would take down her turret canopy, smokestacks, and any other external fittings that might be shot away during a fight.*

CHAPTER SIX

· THE IRONCLADS ·

On March 8, 1862, just days before McClellan began his Peninsular Campaign, the C.S.S. *Virginia*, formerly the U.S.S. *Merrimack*, steamed out of the Elizabeth River into the great harbor of Hampton Roads, Virginia, at the mouth of Chesapeake Bay—and into history. In command was Captain Franklin Buchanan, an aggressive and determined officer who had been John Dahlgren's predecessor as commander of the Washington Navy Yard.

Franklin Buchanan, captain of the Virginia

In the space of a few hours, the *Virginia* demonstrated her absolute technical superiority over the Union ships blockading the Roads. She attacked at will, destroying two major combatant ships and perhaps three transports. At the end of that day, the *Virginia* steamed back to Norfolk, her captain confident that he could finish the job of smashing the Union blockade fleet the next day.

Even in those early days of the war, the effects of Scott's Anaconda Plan were beginning to be felt. The Confederacy was suffering a shortage of everything from rifles to warships, gunpowder to silk dresses. The *Virginia* had been built to end those shortages by breaking the blockade wide open. Once that was done, the Confederacy would be able to sell her cotton to Great Britain and France and to import all the finished manufactured goods the new nation so desperately needed.

The Confederacy would have access to an unending flow of military equipment and supplies as well as morale-raising civilian goods. Success on the battlefield would surely follow. With the military situation vastly improved and with the new trade relationships with the European Powers, diplomatic recognition could not be far behind—and that would force the Union to concede defeat, rather than risk war with Great Britain and France. The Confederate States of America would be accepted as a nation, not just a rebellious section of the United States.

But less than 24 hours later these dreams would go up in smoke. The *Virginia* would be fought to a draw by the U.S.S. *Monitor*, a ship that was as technologically superior to the *Virginia* as the *Virginia* was to the Union ships she had destroyed.

The story of the *Monitor* and the *Virginia* began in the still-dying embers of the Gosport Navy Yard, burned and abandoned by the Union at the very start of the war. Once the Northern forces withdrew, Virginians and Confederates rushed in. They seized vast amounts of equipment and supplies that Union forces had failed to destroy or remove. The frigate *Merrimack* (sometimes spelled *Merrimac*), in the yard for a major refit at the time of the seizure, was the greatest prize. She had burned to the waterline, but the sunken portions of her hull were largely intact, and her worn-out engines were salvageable.

The Confederates decided to make use of the ruined *Merrimack*'s hull as the underlying structure of an iron-clad ship that would be christened C.S.S. *Virginia*. They would patch up her crotchety old steam engine as well, even though the Union navy had planned to junk it.

Stephen R. Mallory had been thinking about building ironclads from the moment he had been named Confederate Navy Secretary. The South was short of almost everything such ships required. But when the *Merrimack* was raised, he knew they were suddenly more than halfway toward having an ironclad ship. Mallory, a pre-secession U.S. Senator from Florida, had served on the Committee on Naval Affairs. He knew what ships the U.S. Navy had—and that the North had no ironclads under construction.

In the North, rumors that the South might be building an armored ship began to shake Secretary of the Navy Gideon Welles out of his complacency about ironclads. In early May 1861, Welles had turned down the chance to buy iron suitable for ironclads. But the news that the Rebels were building an ironclad in Gosport Navy Yard, in Norfolk, changed his mind.

The Union navy, supported by the guns of Fortress Monroe, controlled the mouth of Chesapeake Bay. Welles knew that the ships blockading that area were the cork in a bottle, sealing the Confederate naval forces inside the mouth of Hampton Roads. But if a Confederate ironclad managed to uncork the bottle, Southern naval ships and merchantmen could come and go as they pleased. Welles had to act. By August, Welles had the legal authority—and the money—to build ironclad ships. Even so, Mallory got in three month's work on his ship before the Union responded.

On September 19, a businessman named Cornelius Bushnell, seeking technical advice on another type of ship, consulted engineer John Ericsson. Ericsson showed him his plans for an ironclad ship that could be built in 90 days. Bushnell promptly took the plans and a small cardboard model to Welles.

Four days after Bushnell first saw Ericsson's plans, Bushnell presented them to the President. Lincoln expressed his approval by saying that he felt "a good deal as the western girl did when she stuck her foot in the stocking…that there was something in it." Four days later, Ericsson's plans were accepted by the government.

Stephen R. Mallory oversaw the conversion of the Merrimack *in the dry dock at Gosport Navy Yard.*

Fear of the Confederate ironclad was behind the fast decision, and two elements of Ericsson's design were calculated to calm those fears: It was an ironclad, and it could be built quickly.

That design was for a ship utterly different from anything that had come before. At the beginning of the war, ships of all the world's navies were made of wood and powered at least in part by wind and sail. By the end of the war, all such ships, in all navies, were completely obsolete.

CONTINUED ON PAGE 56 ☞

· WOODEN SHIPS AND FIGHTING SAIL ·

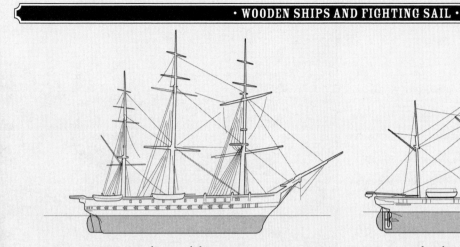

Sail-powered ship

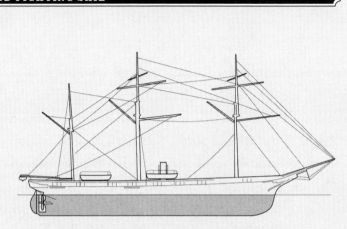
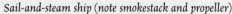

Sail-and-steam ship (note smokestack and propeller)

Every weapon design requires choices about features that are often in conflict with each other. For example, a heavier cannon can usually fire a larger charge without damage to the barrel, but a lighter cannon will be easier to move. A cannon with thick enough walls could handle a huge charge of powder, but it might be too heavy to bring to the battlefield.

Naval architects (people who design ships) have to balance conflicting requirements for war-ships. Ships need speed and fire-power. But 19th-century naval weapons meant cannon, and cannon weigh a lot. Put too many of them on a ship, and their weight will cut into the ship's speed.

Before the Civil War, virtually every warship in the world was made of wood and was propelled either entirely by sail or by a combination of sail and steam engine. Such ships would use sail for long journeys, then shift to steam for close-in operations or to improve speed and maneuverability during a fight. If the steam engine broke, the ship could still sail home.

There were big disadvantages to this arrangement. When a ship was under sail, the steam engine and the tons of coal used to power it were dead weight, slowing down the ship. When the engines were running, all the masts, sails, rigging, and so on were dead weight. There had to be room to carry spare masts and sails as well as fuel and repair parts for the engine. Such ships also needed crew members who could rig sails and engineers who could operate and maintain a steam engine.

The compromises were too great to last. Steam-powered ships replaced sail-and-steam ships as soon as steam engines became more powerful and reliable.

Many early steam-powered ships relied on paddlewheels, not propellers, for propulsion. But the sidewheels or stern-wheels on these ships were big targets as well as fragile and hard

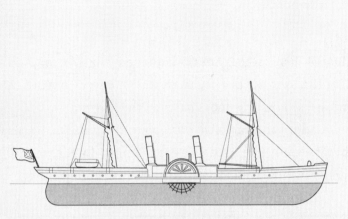

Steam-powered sidewheeler

Two steam-and-sail ships exchange broadside shots.

to protect from incoming fire.

By whatever means they were propelled, pre-Civil War fighting ships were all built—and all fought—in more or less the same way. They carried muzzleloaded cannon set in fixed positions along each side of the ship and placed well outboard to avoid interfering with the sails, masts, and rigging. The big guns could be run in and out on wheels or rails for reloading during a fight. They could be aimed higher or lower, but generally their aim could not be shifted very much from side to side.

The ideal way for a captain to use these ships in a fight was to chase down his opponent, come up alongside, and fire a broadside—all the guns on one side of the ship going off at once.

If the enemy had enough sail on and was making a hard turn, his ship might be heeled over (leaning over to one side because of the force of the wind or the turn), exposing parts of the hull that were normally under the waterline. So, if the attacker was lucky, he could shoot into the ship's exposed section. Once the targeted ship completed its turn and the hull leveled out, the water would rush into the holes below the waterline. Sometimes, an attacker might try a shot intended to wreck his enemy's steering by smashing her rudder or the mechanism connecting it to the ship's wheel.

At any given time, at least half of a ship's guns would be out of the fight. And, if one ship were in position to fire a broadside into the side of another ship, that pretty much meant the other ship was in position to fire a broadside right back.

As the centuries passed, ships got faster, guns got better, and there were improvements in the design, manufacture, and use of sail. But, by the time of the Civil War, the basics of naval warfare hadn't changed that much since the British Royal Navy fought off the Spanish Armada in 1588.

As fall turned to winter, the shipyards of North and South plunged into an arms race, with both sides well aware that the other side was working as fast as it could. In New York, the work of building the *Monitor* was shared by several ironworks and shipyards in order to speed things up. They were racing against the clock to finish the *Monitor* before the South launched the *Virginia*. In Virginia, as many as 1,500 men at a time were at work in and around the dry dock that held the *Virginia*.

Mallory and his team struggled to get the materials they needed. The Tredegar Iron Works, in Richmond, somehow managed to salvage and reuse enough iron to

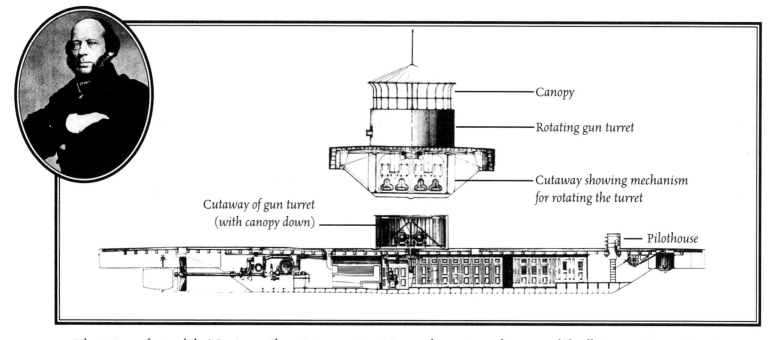

Canopy

Rotating gun turret

Cutaway showing mechanism for rotating the turret

Cutaway of gun turret (with canopy down)

Pilothouse

John Ericsson designed the Monitor with a rotating gun turret to provide maximum firepower while offering a minimum target area.

clad the ship. Much of it was recovered from the wreckage left behind when the Union forces burned Gosport Navy Yard, and more came from surplus railroad iron and disused trolley tracks. Making the armor was not the only problem. With supplies of spare parts and new machinery from the North cut off since the start of the war, the Confederate rail network was already so worn and in need of repair that some armor shipments had to be routed from Richmond through North Carolina and back north into Virginia in order to reach Norfolk.

The race to build the ships in effect ended in a tie. The *Virginia* was completed after the *Monitor,* but both ships had major flaws that required more work. Steering problems caused the *Monitor* to crash into a dock on her first trials. An inexperienced officer blasted her two guns off their mountings during test firings.

The builders of the *Virginia* discovered that her armor made her so top-heavy that she could easily capsize. They put 200 tons of ballast in the bottom of the ship. That made her more stable but also slowed her down and made her ride lower in the water. Her draft (the measure of how far down in the water the lowest part of a ship goes) was 22 feet. This meant she could only operate in water deeper than that. By contrast, the *Monitor*'s draft was less than 12 feet.

Ericsson and his partners had promised to deliver the *Monitor* by mid-January. By the time Ericsson patched up the steering and had the guns remounted, he was almost a month late, but the *Monitor* was nearly ready for sea.

Toward the end of February, a freed slave who was a housekeeper for one of the engineers working on the *Virginia* overheard him talking about the progress being made. At great risk, she made her way from Norfolk to Washington and was ushered into Gideon Welles's office. She reported that the *Virginia* was fully armored, that her guns were being fitted, and that stores were being loaded aboard. On February 20, Welles ordered the *Monitor*—still not officially commissioned as a Union navy ship, still without a crew, still without her sea trials completed—to sail south to confront the *Virginia.*

The *Monitor* left New York on March 6. Not designed for the open ocean, she had to be towed south through

rough seas. Design flaws, construction mistakes, and an inexperienced crew put her in deadly peril. On this her maiden voyage she almost sank twice.

On March 8, while the *Monitor* was still at sea, the C.S.S. *Virginia* cast off her lines to begin her first trials. Her captain, Franklin Buchanan, waited until they were underway to let it be known that it was not to be a mere shakedown cruise. He was sailing right into battle. He set a course straight for his first intended victim, the U.S.S. *Cumberland*. The *Cumberland* was a sailing ship without steam power. As the *Virginia* came toward her, she was sitting at anchor with her sails furled and laundry drying in the rigging. She had no chance of escaping the *Virginia*. "[W]e saw what to all appearances looked like the roof of a very large barn belching forth smoke as from a chimney on fire," wrote one Union officer. The *Virginia* commenced firing with her bow gun. The *Cumberland* answered with broadside after broadside that had no effect. The nearby U.S.S. *Congress* fired as well.

The *Virginia*'s bow-gun fire killed and wounded many of the *Cumberland*'s crew, while the ironclad's starboard guns wrecked a *Congress* cannon, killing or wounding the entire gun crew. More shots pierced her hull, started fires, and killed the ship's commander. The *Virginia*'s ram smashed into the *Cumberland*. Sinking, the Union ship fired repeated broadsides at point-blank range. At that short distance, her fire was able to crack, though not break through, the *Virginia*'s armor. The *Cumberland* went to the bottom. One hundred twenty-one of her crew were dead.

The *Virginia* now turned her attention to the *Congress*, another sailing ship with no auxiliary steam engine. Buchanan ordered his crew to fire on her, and they did, with deadly efficiency.

With her commander and a quarter of the crew dead, she quickly surrendered. Under the rules of war, the *Congress* was Buchanan's legal prize and could no longer offer resistance. But the Union army troops on the land behind the *Congress* had not surrendered. They fired on smaller Confederate craft moving in to take off survivors from the *Congress*. Infuriated, Buchanan grabbed a gun, went up on deck, and starting firing back at the soldiers on the shore. A Union bullet caught him in the thigh.

With Buchanan wounded, the *Virginia's* executive officer took command.

Leaving the *Congress* to burn, he attacked the next target: the nearby U.S.S. *Minnesota*, a steam frigate (a sailing ship equipped with steam engines) that had run aground in the shallow waters while attempting to engage the *Virginia*. However, night was drawing on, and the tide was dropping—something that the *Virginia*, with her 22-foot draft, had to worry about.

She withdrew, confident that she would return in the morning and finish her work of wrecking the Union fleet. No one aboard the *Virginia* could have known what would be waiting for them the next day.

At about 9 p.m., after a harrowing voyage down the coast, the *Monitor* entered the waters of Hampton Roads. For most aboard, there had been no sleep for much of the last two stormy days. Maneuvering by the light of the burning *Congress*, she dropped anchor near the grounded *Minnesota*, and her exhausted crew prepared for battle.

CONTINUED ON PAGE 62 ☞

· THE VIRGINIA'S RAM ·

The *Virginia* boasted a new weapon that was thousands of years old: an iron ram fixed to her bow. Romans rowed their ships in battle and attacked by ramming enemy vessels. Sailing ships could not ram. With attacker and target ships both wind-propelled, the attacker could not build up enough closing speed. Besides, a sailing ship trying to ram an enemy could not bring her broadside guns to bear, but the defending ship could. Steam power and iron shielding made ramming possible again. The attack on the *Cumberland* by the *Virginia* was the first test of this new—and ancient—tactic.

The Virginia *rams the* Cumberland.

· MONITOR & VIRGINIA: NEW WAYS TO FIGHT ·

The Virginia *rode so low that a crewman on her main deck appeared to be standing on the water.*

The battle between the *Virginia* and the *Monitor* was the first ship-to-ship fight to test three major innovations in warship design. The *Virginia* had two of these innovations, while the *Monitor* had all three.

The first was getting rid of sail power altogether and relying on underwater screws (also called propellers). If the ship didn't have sails, an enemy ship couldn't cripple her by shooting them away, and no crewmen needed to climb the rigging and expose themselves to fire. A propeller-driven ship could move in any direction with little concern about the strength or direction of the wind, and it could change speed and direction simply by running the engine faster or slower or by changing the rudder angle without having to shift sails.

The second was the iron plating. (The *Monitor* was all metal, but many later ironclads had hulls or decks or other important elements made of wood.) This armor allowed an ironclad to deflect cannonballs without significant damage. It was not just a matter of slapping iron over an existing ship, however. Though they took different approaches, the designers of both the *Monitor* and the *Virginia* worked to reduce the size of the target by limiting exposed surfaces, and they used curved shapes to help deflect shots, so that cannonballs would slide off and past the ship instead of striking squarely into it.

Both ships paid a price for this protection. The armor plating made the ships very heavy, very slow, and very hard to maneuver. They were not capable of independent operations in the open ocean. They were really only suited to work on rivers and in more protected coastal waters.

The third innovation was the gun turret the *Monitor* had— and the *Virginia* did not. This heavily armored, 120-ton cylinder was turned by auxiliary steam engines (*see page 56*). The turret had two gun doors through

This 1862 illustration shows the Monitor *with canopy and smokestacks up—sailing backwards!*

which her twin 11-inch Dahlgren smoothbore cannon fired 180-pound solid iron balls.

The gun turret changed naval warfare even more than screw propulsion or armor. With a turret, a captain no longer had to aim his ship to aim the gun. He could fire at a target in front of him, behind him, or to either side with equal ease. The turreted gun could track a target, keeping it under fire as the ship maneuvered.

The partially experimental *Monitor* did not quite live up to this ideal of unrestricted fire. The guns could not fire directly over the bow for fear that the shock wave from the cannon blast might stun and incapacitate sailors in the small pilot-house near the bow of the ship. Some people believed it was also dangerous to fire directly astern, over the boilers of her steam engine. The boilers were under high pressure already, and the shock and blast of the guns might be enough to pop them open. By one calculation, the *Monitor* could fire safely over only 200 degrees of a 360-degree circle—but even that was a vast improvement on the fixed guns of older designs.

The *Virginia* and many steam-and-sail ships did have guns mounted on special circular tracks that allowed the gun's aim to be shifted to a limited degree. These pivot guns were so large and heavy that an entire gun crew was needed to manhandle them into position. Generally speaking, they could not be shifted quickly or easily, or aimed independently of the ship. The *Virginia* had a bow pivot gun that could be shifted, by muscle-power, to fire through gun ports aimed either straight ahead or about 45 degrees to port or to starboard. Her stern pivot had a similar arrangement. But in order to fire her main guns, she had to turn sideways to the target and fire broadside—exactly the same way wooden ships had done it for hundreds of years.

By 6:30 a.m. the next day, Lincoln and his Cabinet were already in session, studying increasingly frantic telegraph messages that had come in the previous day and through the night: THE CONGRESS HAS SURRENDERED....I EXPECT TO SEE HER IN FLAMES SOON...WE WANT POWDER BY THE BARREL...THE MERRIMACK [Virginia] HAS IT ALL HER OWN WAY...OUR SAILORS SWIMMING TO SHORE....WE HAVE NO MORE AMMUNITION....[The Virginia] SANK THE CUMBERLAND.... THE MINNESOTA IS AGROUND. THE ST. LAWRENCE JUST ARRIVED....PROBABLY BOTH WILL BE TAKEN...."

Lincoln was deeply worried. Secretary of War Edwin M. Stanton seemed close to panic, predicting that the Virginia "will destroy...every naval vessel; she will lay all the [Northern] cities on the seaboard under contribution [forcing someone to pay, or contribute, ransom or else be destroyed]." He looked out a window that faced the Potomac River. "Not unlikely," he said, "we will have a shell or a cannonball from one of her guns in the White House before we leave this room." Navy Secretary Welles knew that was nonsense, if for no other reason than the Virginia could not make it past the shallowest point of the river.

His suggestion that the Monitor, one tiny ship with only two guns, might still save the day was met with disbelief.

Meanwhile, the Virginia sailed at first light, intent on finishing what she had started the day before. As she moved closer to her next intended target, the Minnesota, her men saw something strange in the water. One of them wrote: "[W]e thought at first it was a raft on which one of the Minnesota's boilers was being taken to shore for repair." Another Confederate officer described it as "an immense shingle floating in the water, with a gigantic cheese box rising from its center; no sails, no wheels, no smokestacks, no guns. What could it be?...As the Virginia steamed down upon the Minnesota, the cheese box and shingle steamed out to meet her. It was...the Monitor, and then and there commenced the first combat that had ever taken place between ironclads."

Captain John L. Worden, commander of the Monitor, under orders to protect the Minnesota, positioned his vessel between the frigate and the Virginia. He commenced firing at the Confederate ironclad at about 8 a.m. The two ships blasted away at each other for about two hours, but

neither seemed able to do serious harm to the other.

At 10:05, the *Monitor* broke off the action to transfer ammunition from her lower decks to the turret, a procedure that required the turret to be stationary. Worden ordered the ship into shallow water where the *Virginia* could not follow. The *Virginia* then tried to attack the *Minnesota* but instead ran aground.

The battling ironclads failed in their ramming attempts. The Monitor *missed, and the* Virginia *scored only a glancing blow.*

The *Virginia*, taking on water from damage caused by ramming the *Cumberland* and with engines faltering, was facing even greater peril. In running aground, she had exposed the area below her waterline that was not armored. She was still under fire from the *Monitor*, and a lucky shot could have wrecked her. Finally, by pushing her tired old engines to the limit, the *Virginia* managed to free herself.

She attacked the *Monitor* again, and the fight continued, still without any clear result, until a lucky shot from the *Virginia*'s stern gun smashed directly into the *Monitor*'s pilothouse, temporarily blinding the captain. Injured and believing his ship to be badly damaged, he ordered his ship to withdraw into shallow water in order to assess the damage. He ordered his executive officer, Lieutenant Samuel Dana Greene, to take command. Greene quickly concluded that the *Monitor* was still fit for battle.

But the *Virginia* faced another enemy: the ebbing tide. Needing to get home before she was again stranded by low water, the *Virginia* withdrew. Both ships decided the other had given up the fight. Both withdrew, claiming victory. The modern consensus calls it a draw, and viewed on a tactical level, that is a fair assessment.

After the fight, men of the Monitor *view the battle damage. Shots fired by the* Virginia's *cannon barely dented her turret.*

Neither ship managed to sink the other, but after-action examination of the ships revealed that each did more damage to the other than was apparent during the battle—enough to show that either could have been victorious if luck had gone a different way.

But in a larger, strategic sense, the *Monitor*—and the Union—were the clear winners. The Union ironclad had prevented the *Virginia* from breaking the blockade. The stalemate served as well as a victory in wrecking Confederate prospects of renewed trade, importation of weapons and supplies, diplomatic recognition from France and Britain, and even ultimate victory in the war.

The *Monitor* and the *Virginia* set the pattern for all the ironclads that would come after them. The Union would build dozens of these ships of gradually improving design.

The Confederacy would build far fewer ironclads, and most of them would be "homemade" ships, built using whatever sort of wood was easy to get and iron scrounged from wherever it could be found.

But the ironclads also broke a pattern that otherwise held true. Virtually all the other new technologies used in the Civil War—the telegraph, the railroad, the techniques of mass production, and others—had existed before the war. What was new was that they were used as tools of war. For example, there had been railroads in one form or another for decades, but the Civil War was the first time American trains were used for rapid troop transport and to supply an army in battle.

The ironclads were different. Though inspired by previous military development, they were totally new.

Encasing a ship in armor plate was a purely military technology, with little or no application to civilian purposes.

The ironclads were unique in another way: They were developed during the war, their designs were driven by the events of the war—and they played a major part in fighting the war. None of the other would-be wonder-weapons invented after the start of the conflict were ready in time to change the course of battle.

Every present-day surface combat ship in the world has armor plating, motorized propulsion, and turreted guns that can be aimed independent of the direction of the ship. The *Monitor* is the proud ancestor of them all.

About two months after the battle between the *Monitor* and the *Virginia*, Lincoln, frustrated by the lack of progress in McClellan's Peninsular Campaign, decided to pay a visit to McClellan's base at Fortress Monroe. McClellan was away, overseeing other operations.

Lincoln, knowing that the Confederates were retreating at the time, was surprised to discover there was no plan for recapturing Norfolk and Gosport Navy Yard. He decided to take on the job himself. He even boarded a tug to do some personal reconnoitering and went ashore at a beach he judged to be suitable for a landing. (The actual landing would be elsewhere.)

On May 9, 1862, as Confederates continued their retreat toward Richmond and Union forces were gaining control of the waters around Norfolk and Hampton Roads, the *Monitor* was approached by a vessel carrying a surprise passenger. "[H]is Excellency the President came alongside this morning," the captain of the *Monitor* later wrote. Lincoln wanted to put the *Monitor* to use. "He directed me to proceed on a reconnaissance of the works at Sewell's Point which we had engaged yesterday, to ascertain whether those works had been abandoned or reenforced [sic]....I was to proceed as soon as I completed coaling."

Less than a year before, Lincoln had held a cardboard model of the *Monitor* in his hand. He fought nearly all of his war by making speeches, running meetings, making deals, signing papers, sending telegrams, and waiting in the telegraph office for news to click and clatter in over the wire. Almost always he was far from the events themselves.

As Union forces advanced on Norfolk, the crew of the Virginia *was forced to destroy their ship.*

the crash and rattle of coal being loaded below deck. He could send her off to do his bidding with a gesture and a word of command. It was a moment with a satisfying sense of things coming full circle—of things falling into place.

Soon after, the Commander in Chief had the pleasure of recapturing Norfolk. Less than two days after his encounter with the *Monitor*, the crew of the *Virginia* blew up their ship to prevent her from being captured by advancing Union forces—and President Lincoln, by directly ordering and overseeing the capture of Norfolk, had had a hand in that, too.

But in that moment, he could see the ship that he had helped call into being. He could speak with her captain, note the cannonball-shaped dents and dings in her turret that were the scars of her duel with the *Virginia*, and hear

SUMMER 1862 - SPRING 1863
· LINCOLN SEARCHES FOR A GENERAL ·

· JULY 1862 ·

● McClellan's Peninsular Campaign collapses in failure. In its aftermath, Lincoln removes nearly all the troops from McClellan's command. They are transferred to northern Virginia and placed under Brigadier General John Pope's Army of Virginia.

· AUGUST 28-30, 1862 ·

● Pope, leading an army of 75,000 men, is defeated by a Confederate army of 55,000 under Generals Stonewall Jackson and James Longstreet at the Battle of Second Bull Run (Manassas) in northern Virginia. The Union army retreats to Washington. Lincoln relieves Pope.

· SEPTEMBER 1, 1862 ·

● Lincoln reluctantly appoints McClellan to command the defense of Washington, saying "We must use what tools we have. There is no man in the Army who can lick these troops into shape half as well as he can."

· SEPTEMBER 17, 1862 ·

● McClellan fights Lee to a draw at Antietam (Sharpsburg), in Maryland. He fails to pursue the Southern army back into Virginia.

· SEPTEMBER 22, 1862 ·

● Lincoln claims Antietam as a Union victory and uses it as an occasion to issue the preliminary Emancipation Proclamation, freeing slaves in areas in rebellion effective January 1, 1863.

· NOVEMBER 1862 ·

● After the Congressional election in the fall of 1862, Lincoln fires McClellan again and appoints Major General Ambrose Burnside in his place.

· DECEMBER 11-15, 1862 ·

● Burnside orders uphill frontal assaults that cost thousands of lives and suffers a brutal defeat at the hands of Lee's army at the Battle of Fredericksburg, in Virginia. Burnside retreats across the Rappahannock River, ending the Union offensive.

· JANUARY 20-22, 1863 ·

● Burnside's second attempt to attack Lee is ruined by bad weather and comes to be known as the Mud March.

· JANUARY 26, 1863 ·

● Major General Joseph Hooker replaces Burnside.

· APRIL 30-MAY 6, 1863 ·

● Hooker loses his nerve and is outflanked by the Confederates at the Battle of Chancellorsville, in Virginia, in what is called "Lee's perfect battle." But Stonewall Jackson is accidentally shot by his own men.

· EARLY JUNE 1863 ·

● Lee begins his second invasion of the North. Lincoln decides Hooker's response is not aggressive enough. Days before the Battle of Gettysburg, Lincoln appoints Major General George Gordon Meade to command the Army of the Potomac.

A Union navy gun crew struggles in a storm, taking aim at a blockade runner. The runners timed their runs to cross the blockade line on moonless nights. Bad weather could also help them hide.

CHAPTER SEVEN

· RUNNERS & RAIDERS ·

On April 2, 1863, women, fed up with shortages and impossibly high prices, marched on the business section of Richmond, Virginia, and began looting the stores. They demanded that the merchants sell at what the women thought were fair prices. When the merchants refused, the women took what they wanted. Their main demand was for food, but soon the looting expanded to attacks on dress shops and jewelry stores.

Southern women in Richmond's bread riot

The rioters were shocked to see President Jefferson Davis leap to the back of a horse cart and call out to them, "[W]e do not desire to injure anyone, but this lawlessness must stop. I will give you five minutes to disperse, otherwise you will be fired upon." Then an officer ordered soldiers to load their weapons. Five minutes later the street was empty, but the riots spread to other cities before subsiding.

The riots were about more than citizens being angry at high prices. Before the war the South had sold its crops to the world and had relied on the world to sell it everything else it needed—an arrangement that left it dependent on outsiders, especially the North. The Southern writer James B. D. DeBow summed up the situation: "Our slaves work with Northern hoes, ploughs, and other implements. The slaveholder dresses in Northern goods, rides in a Northern saddle…reads Northern books.…In Northern vessels his products are carried to market…and on Northern-made paper, with a Northern pen, with Northern ink, he resolves and re-resolves in regard to his rights."

By April 1863, every state in the Confederacy was experiencing shortages of food, clothing, weapons, farm equipment, and nearly everything else. The shortages were worsened by disruptions to every form of transporta-

· CONFEDERATE SHORTAGES ·

During the war, the South was forever robbing Peter to pay Paul. There was a shortage of just about everything. Meeting one need almost always meant doing without something else.

Matthew Fontaine Maury, one of the leading scientists of the Confederacy, performed extensive experiments with torpedoes, which would be called mines today. It was said that such torpedoes sank more Union ships than any other means of attack. They were an important weapon, and developing them was a priority. But when Maury needed insulated wire in order to explode the weapons with electricity, there was none to be had. In fact, there was no wire factory or source of suitable insulation anywhere in the Confederacy.

Maury risked sending an agent into enemy territory— all the way to New York—just to buy insulated wire, but even that attempt failed. He finally got the wire he needed from another source. He scavenged leftovers from a failed Union attempt to run an underwater cable across Chesapeake Bay.

Even people were in short supply. At one time skilled workmen were taken from the Tredegar Iron Works to serve in a defense battalion, which reduced the number of cannon Tredegar could produce.

British observer Lieutenant Colonel Arthur James Lyon Fremantle told Confederate officials "your system feeds upon itself." He was talking about its military officers, but he could have been speaking about the whole Southern economy. It lurched from shortage to shortage, patching up and making do, with scarcely the time or money needed to make anything new or do anything properly.

tion, by turning farmers into soldiers, and by the loss of vitally needed slave labor, as more and more black men and women escaped into the Northern lines. But the blockade was the main cause for the logistical nightmares that plagued the Confederacy. Something had to be done.

At the start of the war, when the Union was scrambling to get enough ships together to cover all the ports, the blockade was largely ineffective. Just about any ship stood a good chance of making it through the cordon, and the incentives to make the attempt were great. Captains could turn huge wartime profits while taking little actual risk.

Outbound, the chief cargo was cotton. The blockade-running ships were described in terms of how many bales of cotton they could carry. As was true before the war, the plan was for the export of cotton and other agricultural products to pay for virtually all Southern imports.

Inbound, the runners played a vital role in supplying the Confederates with military supplies—everything from rifles to saltpeter for making gunpowder, from paper for making cartridges to the lead for making bullets. Over the course of the war, for example, 700,000

The British-built Robert E. Lee *made 21 voyages in 10 months. She carried a total of 7,000 bales of cotton outbound and vital munitions inbound before her capture and conversion into a Union blockade ship.*

Enfield rifles manufactured in Britain were brought in.

The runners also carried foodstuffs—coffee, beef, and pork—as well as luxury goods, such as liquor and fashionable clothing. Prices were astronomically high at both ends, and the profits from only two successful runs could be equal to the value of the ship carrying the cargo.

Many blockade runners were built in Britain and belonged to private businesses rather than the Confederate government. Sidewheelers with auxiliary sails and screw sloops (sailing ships that had steam-driven propellers, sometimes called screws) did good service. Runners were custom-built so they could move through shallow water and had special features that made them hard to spot.

To keep clouds of excess steam from escaping into the air and revealing the ship's position, runners ran special steam-relief lines underwater. They burned anthracite coal because it gave off almost no smoke. Removing sails and yards (horizontal support beams) made them harder to see, as did their dull paint jobs. They even had telescoping funnels (smokestacks) that could be lowered during their runs, reducing their profiles even more. It was 19th-century stealth technology.

*A Northern cartoon shows
a piratical Rafael Semmes.*

But despite these innovations, more and more blockade runners were getting caught. Navy Secretary Mallory decided to attack Northern shipping in hopes of forcing the blockaders to withdraw to deal with the trouble. If Union ships were forced to chase Southern raiders all over the ocean, that would mean fewer vessels on blockade duty.

The Confederacy bought British-made commerce raiders that, by targeting merchant ships, would disrupt the Union's trade with the rest of the world. The raiders were mostly wooden-hulled, steam-and-sail fighting ships. They could be built but not armed in Britain because that country's proclamation of neutrality forbade any British shipyards "to equip, furnish, fit out or arm" warships for the North or the South. To get around this restriction, guns and ammunition were added after the "civilian" ship left British waters.

The most famous of these commerce raiders began construction as Hull No. 290 and was launched on July 28, 1862, using the cover name *Enrica*. Three weeks later, after being outfitted for war on an island in the mid-Atlantic, her captain, Rafael Semmes, raised the Rebel naval ensign above his ship for the first time. She sailed into international waters under her proper name, C.S.S. *Alabama*, on August 24, 1862.

Semmes and his ship sailed the oceans of the world for the next 21 months— attacking whatever Union merchant vessels he could find. She took more than 60 prizes, as captured ships were called. She also sank the U.S.S. *Hatteras*, earning her the distinction of being the only Confederate ship to defeat a Union warship on the high seas. She caused an uproar in the Northern merchant fleet, and, as Mallory had expected, the Union navy was forced to send ships in pursuit of her and the other raiders.

The *Alabama* never touched the shore of North America. After remaining almost continuously at sea for the better part of two years, the *Alabama* put into port at Cherbourg, France, on June 11, 1864, for repairs. Alert Union diplomats, seeing a chance to capture the raider,

The crew of the U.S.S. Kearsarge *rejoices as the C.S.S.* Alabama *lowers her flag and surrenders off the coast of Cherbourg, France.*

contacted John A. Winslow, captain of the U.S.S. *Kearsarge,* which was sailing in Dutch waters. He immediately sailed for the French port, arriving on June 14.

On Sunday, June 19, 1864, a curious crowd gathered on the docks, on the shore, and on boats at sea to watch the battle between the two ships. All of the advantages were with the *Kearsarge.* A little more than an hour later the *Alabama* was sinking, with massive holes in her side.

Other Confederate commerce raiders were still at large, but none would do as much damage or cause the Union navy to divert as many resources from the blockade as the *Alabama.*

But whatever the *Alabama* and her sister raiders did was not enough. The blockade still held and was getting stronger. In 1861, nine out of ten attempts to run the blockade had succeeded. By 1865, only one out of two blockade runners would avoid capture. No Confederate army lost a battle because the blockade kept it from getting guns or ammunition. But many a soldier went without shoes or uniforms, and there was scarcely anything the civilian economy did not run out of. The blockade played a major role in bringing the Confederate economy to the brink of complete collapse.

But before the North could win the war, it would have to shatter the last major gateway between the Confederate east and west and then repel a desperate invasion by soldiers seeking the equipment, supplies—and food— they could no longer find in the South.

Confederate Brigadier General Wade Hampton was almost trapped by Union cavalry during a large-scale fight between mounted units—part of the Battle of Gettysburg.

CHAPTER EIGHT

· OLD WAR, NEW WAR ·

In the spring of 1863, two generals who would later confront each other were a thousand miles apart, each intent on invading the other's territory. In the West, Ulysses S. Grant was plotting the downfall of Vicksburg, Mississippi, while in the East, Robert E. Lee was on the road that would lead him to Gettysburg, Pennsylvania. Each general would deal with the old and the new.

It has been said of the American Civil War that it was the last ancient war, and, at the same time, the first modern war; one of the last wars in which massed cavalry units battled against each other, and the first war in which railroads played a major part. By its end, elite units of the Union army carried breech-loaded repeating rifles. But they were led by officers who still wore sabers. For the most part, these swords were no longer weapons.

The telegraph sent word of the fall of Vicksburg.

They were merely elaborately decorated, expensively made, ceremonial pointing sticks. Officers used swords with a range of six feet to direct men armed with rifles that could shoot half a mile.

The old war banged and jostled against the new war in many similar ways—ways that strike a modern reader as odd or even ridiculous. But to the people of the time, all of their world, not just the war, was a jumble of old and new, of horse-drawn carriages and railroads, of medical practices that had barely changed in hundreds of years being used to treat wounds caused by weapons that had just been invented.

The Union army and navy had made gradual, fitful progress in the West in 1862 and the first half of 1863. Union forces controlled the city and port of New Orleans and, thus, the mouth of the Mississippi River as well as large sections of the northern part of the river.

Vicksburg's position astride the twisting turns of the Mississippi gave it huge strategic importance.

But the conquest of the western rivers would not be complete until the Union controlled Vicksburg, Mississippi. It was a key river port, situated on high bluffs overlooking the river, making it a perfectly sited citadel. Vicksburg stood on the eastern shore on a sharp turn of the Mississippi. The city's cannon commanded a vast section of the river. That meant a long stretch of the Mississippi was open for Confederate traffic, both up and down the river—and, perhaps even more important, for traffic across the river.

Vicksburg was the last major link between the eastern and western portions of the Confederacy. Cargo could come in by rail to Vicksburg, be sent across the river by boat, and then be sent off again by rail. Without that link, the Confederate states east of the Mississippi would be cut off from western food supplies, and the western Confederacy would be cut off from the outside world, except for what smugglers might be able to bring in.

As Abraham Lincoln himself had said in the early stages of the war, "See what a lot of land these fellows hold, of which Vicksburg is the key! The war can never be brought to a close until that key is in our pocket." Recalling his own youthful travels riding flatboats down the Mississippi River, the Commander in Chief said, "I am acquainted with that region and know what I am talking about. And as valuable as New Orleans will be to us, Vicksburg will be more so."

Confederate President Jefferson Davis saw the same strategic situation, calling Vicksburg "the nail head that holds the South's two halves together."

Repeated Union attempts to bypass Vicksburg's guns by digging canals failed.

Grant had faced losses and reverses, but he had also marked up victories in Tennessee at Fort Henry and Fort Donelson in February 1862 and in the bloody shambles of the Battle of Shiloh in April 1862. In December 1862 he had been ordered to take Vicksburg. Between that time and March 1863 he made no fewer than seven failed attempts to get through the rivers, bogs, swamps, high bluffs, flooded fields, and high water around the city.

Despite the setbacks, Grant tried again in April. His forces were able to move down the western shore of the river, and Admiral David Porter's Union gunboats could safely operate in the waters north and upstream of the city. But because the guns of Vicksburg looked down from high bluffs, Grant could not attack the city directly.

Grant's latest plan called for Porter's ships to meet up with Grant's troops south of Vicksburg on the western shore, well out of range of the city's guns. From there Porter's ships would ferry Grant's troops across to the eastern shore. A plan relying on such close army-navy cooperation was a novelty.

While Grant worked his troops around the labyrinthine western shore, Porter ran his gunboats and transports past Vicksburg at night. He hoped to get by unseen, but his fleet was detected, and a wild artillery battle lit up the sky. The gunboats took damage but made it past and met up with Grant south of the town of Hard Times, Louisiana, on the western shore of the river.

On April 30, they succeeded in crossing to Bruinsburg on the eastern shore. "When this was effected," Grant later wrote, "I felt a degree of relief scarcely ever equaled since. Vicksburg was not yet taken it is true....I was now in the enemy's country, with a vast river and the stronghold of Vicksburg between me and my base of supplies [in Memphis, Tennessee, about 200 miles north]. But I was on

The Union fleet of gunboats and transports runs past the guns of Vicksburg.
Once downstream, the ships will carry Grant's troops across the river.

dry ground on the same side of the river with the enemy...."

Grant moved north—but not due north toward Vicksburg. Instead he headed northeast, toward Jackson, Mississippi's state capital. He planned to wreck its rail yards to prevent the Confederates from using trains to bring in large numbers of troops against him, the way Brigadier General Johnston had moved against the Union at the First Battle of Bull Run. That very same Johnston was now in charge of troops in Jackson. Lieutenant General John C. Pemberton, commander of the defenses at Vicksburg, sent out forces as well, putting Grant squarely between two Confederate armies. The Union army lunged east, smashed Jackson, and chased off Johnston's forces. Next, they pursued Pemberton's troops back to Vicksburg. The Confederates settled in behind the city's defenses, while Grant proceeded to make several failed attempts to break through them.

On May 22 the time for a military assault was set, not by firing cannon or signaling, but by means of a fixed schedule and synchronized watches. Union army and navy guns cut loose at the same moment in support of an infantry assault. However, the innovative tactic did little good. The city's defenses were too strong.

Grant finally realized that further direct attacks would do nothing more than add to the casualty list. So he went from the modern world of synchronized watches to the most ancient of tactics: a siege. He would surround the city, seal it off from the outside world, and wait until the enemy's supplies ran out.

The Union forces had no siege experience, but they learned quickly. "The soldiers burrowed like gophers and beavers—a spade in one hand and a musket in the other," one who was there recalled. The Confederates were digging as well, with each side trying to get in close to the enemy while keeping safely under cover.

The siege went on for a month and a half as the

This Vicksburg house, caught between Confederate lines and Union siege-line dugouts, survived the fight and still stands today.

trenches snaked toward each other, and the Union forces waited for the Confederates—and the civilians in the city—to be starved out. Conditions in the town were medieval by the end, with sanitation collapsing and dogs vanishing as people ate things they didn't really want to think about. Pemberton surrendered his army and the city on July 4, correctly figuring that on that day of all days, the Union soldiers would be most disposed to treat his people well.

The news reached Lincoln not from the army, but from the navy: a telegram sent by Acting Rear Admiral David D. Porter to Gideon Welles. It read:

[TO] HON. GIDEON WELLES,

SECRETARY NAVY.

SIR: I HAVE THE HONOR TO INFORM YOU THAT VICKSBURG HAS SURRENDERED TO THE U.S. FORCES ON THIS 4TH OF JULY. VERY RESPECTFULLY, YOUR OBEDIENT SERVANT,

D. D. PORTER,

ACTING REAR-ADMIRAL.

Welles immediately rushed the news to the President. The North rightly saw Vicksburg as a hard-fought triumph that delivered the entire length of the Mississippi into Union control. "The Father of Waters again goes unvexed to the sea," Lincoln declared. The President understood the vital strategic importance of cutting off the river and rail links from the Confederates, as well as the economic and political importance of re-opening the whole length of the river for traffic from the Union states. No longer would they have to fear attack from Confederate forces.

A thousand miles to the east, just as Grant's men were settling in for their siege, Lee was leading his men north. One of his goals, which he never achieved, was to take Harrisburg, Pennsylvania, because it was a rail center. Just as seizing Vicksburg would cut off the western Confederacy from the eastern half, control of Harrisburg would cut off a major link between the eastern and western parts of the Union.

Lee also hoped that by scoring a major victory over Lincoln's Army of the Potomac in the North, he could strengthen desires for peace among Northerners, especially those who had already joined antiwar groups. If Lee could destroy the Army of the Potomac while on Union soil, it would be more than a defeat for the North. It would be a humiliation. A defeated Northern army would be unable to stop him from striking at Baltimore, or even Washington. Even if he could not hold Lincoln's capital forever, the mere act of entering the city would add so much to the South's prestige—and ruin Lincoln's

• PHOTOGRAPHY •

Surprisingly, photography had almost no military value in the Civil War era. The Union army did reproduce some maps photographically, but that was about as far as military use went.

Because the exposure times were so long and the chemical processes for developing images were hard to manage, it was almost impossible to take photographs in a hurry. Virtually all the famous battlefield photos were taken *after* the action. There was no way to use photography *before* a battle as an intelligence tool. No photographs were taken from balloons. Nor was it possible to reproduce photos in newspapers. They had to settle for images drawn from photos.

Portraits were difficult. Subjects had to remain motion-

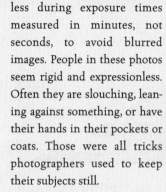

Brady's mobile photographic lab

less during exposure times measured in minutes, not seconds, to avoid blurred images. People in these photos seem rigid and expressionless. Often they are slouching, leaning against something, or have their hands in their pockets or coats. Those were all tricks photographers used to keep their subjects still.

Photographs were shown at exhibitions, and these had a limited but powerful effect. One Mathew Brady exhibit was called "The Dead of Antietam." Oliver Wendell Holmes wrote, "Let him who wishes to know what war is look at this series of illustrations. These wrecks of manhood thrown together in careless heaps ranged in ghastly rows for burial were alive but yesterday."

public standing so completely—that it might force the North to the negotiating table. Lee's goal, in short, was to break the North's will to fight. Some in the North thought it possible to stop the fighting and then reunite the nation through talks and by making concessions.

"Should the belief that peace will bring back the Union become general, the war would no longer be supported," Lee observed, "and that [a loss of support for the war], after all, is what we are interested in bringing about."

Another motive for Lee's move north was to draw the Union armies out of Virginia during the peak of the growing season, so that crops could be harvested. Meanwhile, the Confederate army could re-provision itself off the rich farmland of Pennsylvania.

Lee's army needed supplies. Barefoot men who had walked from Virginia to Pennsylvania were in desperate need of shoes, and there were reports of a supply of them in a nearby town. A Confederate column headed there in an effort to find the rumored shoes, but they were stopped by Union cavalry. This confrontation was the beginning of the Battle of Gettysburg.

A guidon served to locate a unit and its commander on the field. It was a powerfully important symbol. Men would die to protect the colors of their unit.

Gettysburg became a grand-scale version of what is called an encounter battle. Rather than an attacking force moving toward a defending force in a prepared position in a known location, one small group of soldiers encounters another. Both sides summon more and more troops. More and more forces are sucked in until a full-fledged battle develops.

In such a battle, the land being fought on is not the target. The only objective for either side is to smash the opposing army. This was not the gentlemanly old-style war fought between armies for limited objectives. It was a fight to the death.

But even if the invasion of the North was motivated by grimly modern goals, the campaign went forward without the significant use of technology by either side. The men marched toward battle on foot, the officers rode on horseback, and supplies came in via horse-drawn wagon trains. No Union surveillance balloons rose up. Both sides relied on cavalry forces and "scouts" (a polite name for spies) to seek out the enemy, and most routine orders were carried not by telegraph, but by couriers delivering hand-written notes.

When the armies entered the field at Gettysburg, they did so literally with colors (flags) flying, as was the case on both sides throughout the war. Each unit carried its own guidon, or identifying flag. (Pronounced GUY-don, a guidon is a special flag, often either a square or a rectangle with a triangle cut out of one side, giving it a "swallowtail" shape.) Guidons trace their roots to medieval heraldry and the tradition of the royal standard, carried whenever the king was present.

Each soldier could know where his own unit was just by looking for its guidon. Messengers with orders and reports located officers in the same way. Guidons also served as reference points for soldiers to line up in orderly formations. However, they also served as obvious targets for the other side to shoot at. Each side knew the other would not fight as well if its officers were killed in battle, or if the soldier bearing the guidon went down. If that happened, no one could tell which unit was where.

Even without the giant flags that followed them about the field, officers made prime targets. Officers up to and including brigadier generals were expected to risk their lives by leading their men at the front. In earlier wars with shorter-range, less accurate weapons, the risks of leading men from the front had been acceptable. By 1863, the third year of the Civil War, the risks were nearly suicidal. Throughout the war, both Confederate and Union officers were about 15 percent more likely to get killed than enlisted men, and generals were about 50 percent more likely to die than privates. More than once, Confederate soldiers shouted, "General Lee to the rear!" and blocked his horse, preventing him from moving forward.

The system of dealing with prisoners was also caught between old and new. At the start of the Civil War, the two sides relied on a system of paroles and exchanges based on a European tradition: When a soldier was captured, he was expected to promise (or as it was phrased, to give his parole) not to fight again for his side until he was traded, or exchanged, for another prisoner of the same rank. Once he had promised, the parolee might even be allowed to go home to wait for official notice that he had been exchanged.

The old system broke down. Grant was infuriated to discover that some of the 37,000 soldiers captured by the North during the Vicksburg campaign were recaptured in late fall 1863. Paroled Rebels had taken up arms again, even though there had been no exchange of Union prisoners.

The breakdown of the prisoner-parole tradition led to the creation of overcrowded, badly managed prison camps in the North and in the South. Soldiers on both sides dreaded capture and imprisonment. They had little food, drank foul water, and were threatened by deadly diseases that swept through the camps. The worst of the camps was in Andersonville, Georgia, where, in 15 months, nearly 13,000 Union prisoners died. The death rate was also high in many Northern prisons and prison

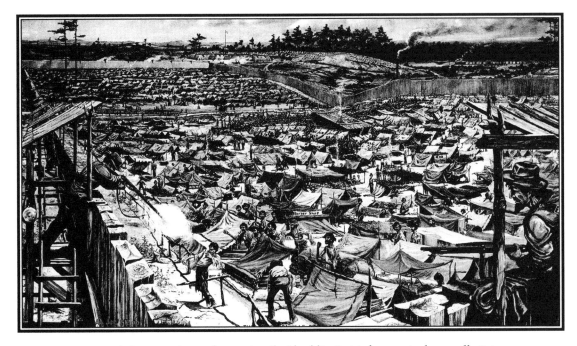

*A guard shoots a prisoner for crossing the "dead line" at infamous Andersonville Prison.
Meant for 10,000, it held 33,000 starving men. Union prisons were little better.*

camps. At one in New York, for example, 775 of the 8,347 prisoners died of disease within a three-month-period. A report on another Northern camp said, "Filth, poor drainage, and overcrowding created a horror. . . ."

The end of the parole system helped to produce what Abraham Lincoln and others referred to as "the arithmetic"—the cold-blooded subtraction of human lives from an army. It is called attrition (the wearing away of something bit by bit). There were more men available to fight for the North than for the South. Therefore, every Southern casualty left a proportionally larger hole in Confederate ranks than a fallen Northern soldier did in Union ranks. And the North was far more able than the South to find new recruits and draftees (soldiers who did not volunteer but were required to perform military service). Simple arithmetic showed that, if the war was fought until one side or the other ran out of men, the South would lose.

Newer ways of fighting were beginning to overtake the old. However, the generals were slow to realize it. At Gettysburg, in what came to be known as Pickett's Charge, 12,000 Confederates attacked across an open field

Pickett's men reach the "High-water Mark of the Confederacy." The South's fortunes receded from that point and never recovered.

toward a defending force of Union soldiers who had dug into prepared positions. Fifty years before, those defenders would have been firing flintlocks similar to the shorter-range, less-accurate weapons used in the Revolutionary War. Against those weapons, Pickett's Charge would have been a grand gesture that might have worked. But the weapons—and the ways of war—had changed, and the charge could not possibly succeed. The Confederate soldiers marched in well-dressed lines, banners flying, all but offering themselves as targets. The Union forces zeroed in on the Confederates, commenced firing, and tore the Southerners to pieces.

A handful of Confederates reached the stone wall that shielded Union troops. There, most were killed, wounded, or captured. It was the farthest north the South ever got—the "High-water Mark of the Confederacy." Lieutenant Colonel Arthur Fremantle of the British Army traveled with the Confederates as a military observer before and during the battle and witnessed the carnage of the fighting. He told one Confederate officer, "You cannot fill the places of these men. Your troops do wonders, but every time at a cost you cannot afford." He, too, understood "the arithmetic."

After the double hammer blows of Vicksburg and Gettysburg, it was no longer possible for the South to win the war on the battlefield. Gettysburg was a turning point in the war, marking the beginning of the end for the South. Confederate soldiers would have to face new and more terrible weapons issuing forth from the workshops and factories of the North, weapons that Lincoln had put in the hands of his Union troops. One of those advanced weapons was the Spencer repeating rifle, and shortly after Gettysburg, the Commander in Chief tested it on the firing range.

A Union sharpshooter takes aim through his precision gun sight in this Winslow Homer illustration. Elite, specially trained sharpshooter units were scheduled to be the first to get breech-loading rifles, but they had to wait months.

CHAPTER NINE

· SLOW MARCH TO RAPID FIRE ·

On August 18, 1863, President Abraham Lincoln strode out into Treasury Park behind the White House. With him was inventor Christopher Spencer. The war news was getting better. Grant had taken Vicksburg in July. Only the week before, Gettysburg's top general, George Gordon Meade, had given Lincoln and his Cabinet a firsthand account of the Union victory in Pennsylvania. The way to an end to the war had begun to seem hopeful.

The Commander in Chief and the inventor were going to try a little target practice with a gun Spencer had designed. Lincoln had known about the Spencer rifle for years and had urged the Army to get them into the field. The Spencer had just seen its first large-scale use in various fights during the Gettysburg campaign and had shown itself to be highly effective.

Lincoln's target board shows good shooting.

Lincoln and Spencer positioned a block of wood to serve as a target and painted a black spot on the center of it. The President raised the gun to his shoulder, took aim, and got off seven quick shots without reloading. His first shot went low, the second struck the bull's-eye, and the last five were closely grouped near the center. Spencer took his turn next and did just a bit better. "Well," the President said evenly, "you are younger than I am, have a better eye, and a steadier nerve."

Who had done the better shooting didn't matter. What did matter was Lincoln's interest in rapid-fire guns and advanced weapons. Some did valuable service during the war. Some were not perfected until after the war ended. Some were not produced due to technical difficulties. Some were turned away for bureaucratic reasons. And some might have changed the course of the war—and of history—if they had been given a chance.

At the start of the Civil War, many of the soldiers, particularly on the Confederate side, armed themselves. Some took down from over their mantelpieces the very same guns their grandfathers and great-grandfathers had used during the Revolutionary War. Others had newer guns made from designs that had not changed much since the Revolution. They were the kind of guns Lincoln had seen used for hunting as a boy.

For the most part these were smoothbore flintlock muzzleloaded guns. (A smoothbore's barrel was drilled, or bored, to form a smooth, polished interior surface.) The flintlock had serious drawbacks, especially as a military weapon. It relied on sparks, produced by striking metal against a flint to set off loose gunpowder in a flash pan (*see page 89*). Those sparks then set off the main firing charge. If the striking mechanism or the powder got wet, the gun was nearly useless. Another drawback was that the powder could spill out of the flash pan. This not only ruined the shot but also could spread a highly flammable substance all over the shooter's clothes and skin.

A new idea, which the U.S. Army accepted in 1842—the percussion cap lock (or cap-lock) firing system—solved just about all these problems. The percussion cap would work in wet weather as long as the gunpowder in the gun barrel was dry. It was mechanically simpler than the flintlock, operated more quickly, and was far more reliable. It also required far less time and attention during the reloading process.

With a percussion-cap system, all the shooter had to do was pull off the old cap and stick on a new one. Best of all, most types of flintlock guns could easily be converted to percussion-cap firing. The switch-over had already started before the Civil War. Not long after the war began, nearly all Confederate and Union troops were carrying converted or newly made percussion-cap guns.

The old method of loading the gun, called muzzleloading (*see page 90*), was much harder to change. The clumsy and complicated process did not matter so much when you were hunting deer or rabbit for dinner. You loaded your weapon, stalked your prey, and fired when you had a chance. But in battle, your targets could shoot back.

· FIRING MECHANISMS ·

FLINTLOCK SYSTEM

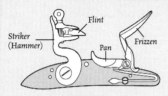

Half cock, frizzen open

To fire a flintlock gun, the shooter first moved the striker to the half-cocked position, flipped the metal frizzen open, and put fine-grain, loose gunpowder in the pan.

Then the shooter closed the frizzen over the pan and the touch hole, (the opening between the pan and the barrel), aimed the gun, and fully cocked the striker.

Full cock, frizzen closed

Pulling the trigger caused the flint in the striker to scrape against the frizzen as it flipped open. Sparks ignited the powder and sent a flash into the touch hole, firing the gun.

Fired

The flintlock firing system was replaced by a mechanism that relied on a cap-shaped object that contained a chemical that would explode when struck hard. It was about the size of a pencil eraser and fit over the top of the nipple that was connected to the touch hole. Pulling the trigger caused the hammer to strike the cap and set off a tiny explosion that traveled through the touch hole, setting off the gunpowder and firing the gun.

PERCUSSION-CAP SYSTEM

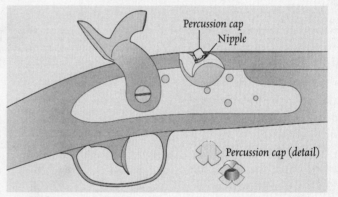

Converting a flintlock (below) so it would fire using percussion caps (above) was a simple process, and many thousands were changed over.

· MUZZLELOADER ·

Loading a muzzleloader was a complicated, multi-step process—
and a dangerous one because standing up made the user a target.

A musket cartridge held ball
and powder in a wrapper.

The term "muzzleloading" refers to a gun that requires the shooter to measure the charge of gunpowder and pour it down the barrel from the muzzle end. A ball-shaped projectile is then dropped down the barrel, so it sits atop the powder. Sometimes a bit of cotton waste or paper or other material is shoved down on top of the ball to hold everything in place. A long metal ramrod is then shoved down the barrel once or twice, to pack everything together.

Muzzleloading relies on gravity, which means that the weapon has to be held upright in order to pour in the powder, drop in the ball (bullet), push in the wadding, and then ram everything home.

Smoothbore muskets typically had gun barrels more than three feet long, which required a ramrod long enough to reach down that far. That, in turn, meant the shooter had to stand while reloading in order to be able to get the ramrod in and out—no problem while hunting game, but often very dangerous in battle.

Things were simplified somewhat by the practice of wrapping a pre-measured charge of gunpowder and a ball in a paper packet called a cartridge. Even so, reloading wasn't fast or easy. After firing, the shooter first had to stand up if he had been firing from a kneeling or prone position. He then had to set the gunstock (the gun's shoulder rest) on the ground. Next, he took a cartridge from the leather cartridge box he carried, tore the end off it with his teeth (because his hands were busy holding the gun barrel and the cartridge) poured the powder into the barrel, dropped the bullet down into the barrel, and likely shoved the paper wrapping down the barrel as well. (The paper wrappers were treated to be highly flammable, so they would burn up quickly and not jam the gun when it went off.) The shooter would then remove the ramrod from the "pipes" (supports that held the ramrod under the gun barrel), ram the cartridge down firmly into the barrel, return the ramrod to the pipes, lift the gun to the firing position, half-cock the gun, remove the old percussion cap from the firing mechanism, take a percussion cap from a special leather carrying pouch, place it on the nipple of the gun, pull the hammer back to the fully cocked position, aim the gun—and then pull the trigger, firing the gun.

Standing up to reload your gun meant you had to expose yourself to enemy fire after every shot.

Soldiers in battle were expected to load and fire three times a minute, while getting off aimed shots. Not all of them managed it. In the stress of battle, a soldier might fire his gun with the ramrod still in the barrel. Some soldiers loaded and reloaded—and then reloaded again and again, without ever firing their weapons. More than 12,000 guns with multiple loads in them were found on the Gettysburg battlefield after the fighting ended. One had more than 23 loads jammed into the barrel.

Smoothbore guns could not shoot very far or very accurately. "At the distance of a few hundred yards," Ulysses S. Grant wrote, "a man [with a flintlock smoothbore] might fire at you all day without your finding it out." The guns were so inaccurate that many did not have a rear sight, as there was no hope of firing accurately enough to need one. A smoothbore required a round projectile (*see page 90*) because a cylindrical bullet would instantly begin tumbling end-over-end as soon as it left the gun barrel. This tumbling would ruin the accuracy of

the shot and produce a lot of air resistance that would slow the bullet, greatly reducing its range. A ball-shaped bullet couldn't tumble.

A rifle—a gun with a long, rifled gun barrel—solved many of these problems. Rifling was the process of making long spiral grooves along the inside of a gun barrel. The bullet engaged with these grooves as it moved down the barrel, and, guided by the spirals, started spinning along an axis at right angles to the direction it was shot. This stabilized the bullet after it left the gun and prevented it from tumbling while in the air. The bullet could fly straighter and farther.

The bullet had to match up precisely with the grooves and fit perfectly into the rifle barrel. Sometimes the shooter, loading the rifle from the muzzle end, had to use a mallet, pounding on the ramrod to force the bullet all the way down the barrel. But too tight a fit could jam the round in the barrel when the gun was fired, causing the rifle to explode in the shooter's face.

The answer was the Minié ball, named for the French military inventor Claude-Étienne Minié. He came up with the basic idea, but it was later improved upon at the U.S. Armory at Harpers Ferry (*see page 93*). Despite its name, it was actually shaped much like a modern bullet—a short, stumpy cylinder rounded at the front. The secret to its success was a hollow, cup-shaped opening at its back end. A Minié ball dropped down loosely and easily into a rifled barrel. When the gun was fired, the soft, thin lead of that cup-shaped opening expanded outward, gripping firmly into the rifled walls of the gun barrel and forming a tight seal between the Minié ball and the rifle barrel. The Minié ball left the barrel spinning along its long axis, in effect drilling itself through the air.

The Springfield Model 1861 rifled musket and the British-made Enfield rifled musket were both muzzle-loaders, and both used Minié balls. Many more than two million of these weapons saw service in the Civil War—on both sides. The British and other foreign powers sold to both North and South. And throughout the war, the Confederacy armed itself in large part by seizing weapons intended for the Union army as well as by scavenging weapons abandoned on the field of battle.

Because they could shoot bullets farther and more accurately than flintlocks, muzzleloaded rifled muskets changed the tactical calculations that officers had learned in their studies of Napoleon's classic warfare at West Point Military Academy. Those tactics were designed for soldiers using flintlock smoothbores against soldiers armed with similar weapons.

Because smoothbores could not shoot far or accurately, attackers could advance to within about 100 yards, attach bayonets, fire one last volley, and then charge the defenders, using their bayoneted guns as spears or clubs.

Defenders might be able to get off one shot each and then try to reload in the 20 or 30 seconds or so it might take the attackers to cover that 100 yards. And, given the firing delays that some flintlocks had, the defenders would have trouble hitting moving targets. This meant attackers had a chance to cross the distance before the defenders could shoot more than once.

The longer-range and more accurate rifled musket changed that calculation drastically, to the advantage of the defenders. Attackers had to start their charge from farther

· TYPES OF BULLETS ·

Of all the weapons and inventions of the Civil War, the Minié ball likely had the most misleading and confusing name. Though the inventor's name was pronounced min-AY, American soldiers pronounced the word as if it were spelled "minnie."

The Minié ball used in the Civil War was an improvement on Minié's design developed by James H. Burton at the U.S. Armory at Harpers Ferry. Despite the name, the Minié or "mini" ball wasn't small or ball-shaped.

It was called a "ball" because most of the ammunition that had come before it was ball-shaped. It was really a short, fat cone. It was more than a half inch in diameter and made of more than an ounce of soft lead, making it about twice the weight of the largest present-day .45 caliber round. The Minié ball was packed in a paper wrapper, or cartridge, along with a pre-measured amount of gunpowder.

The cartridge for the Sharps rifle was a paper or linen cylinder filled with gunpowder. The

bullet was stuck into its top end. The shooter slid the entire cartridge—wrapper, powder, and bullet—into the breech. Closing the breech sliced off the base of the cartridge, exposing the gunpowder so it could be touched off by the percussion cap, which was still a separate item.

The Spencer cartridge was one of the earliest examples of

the modern, all-metal cartridge bullet. The cylinder holding the powder was made of metal, and the base of the cartridge had the percussion cap built into it. There have been many refinements, improvements, and variations, but the basic design of the modern cartridge bullet remains unchanged from the day when Lincoln fired a Spencer rifle.

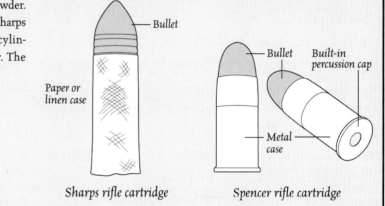

Harpers Ferry Minié ball with cross-section (right)   *Sharps rifle cartridge*   *Spencer rifle cartridge*

back to keep outside the range of the defenders' guns. Instead of taking perhaps 30 seconds to reach the defenders, attackers might need a minute or longer. That interval, along with faster-loading guns, gave the defenders time to

fire two or three times. If you were a defender with a line of men moving toward you, missing one of them likely meant hitting another. An attacker who had to stop and reload while in range of the defenders made himself a target. And if he did not reload midway across the field, he could fire exactly once as he advanced, provided he had managed to reload just before getting the order to charge.

When all these facts are combined together, the grim result explains why virtually every frontal charge by infantry units in the Civil War failed. Nearly always, the attackers suffered massive casualties and failed to take the defenders' position.

About 12,000 Union soldiers were killed or wounded in Virginia at the Battle of Fredericksburg (December 1862), about 8,000 of them in repeated, hopeless direct assaults on Maryes Heights. Pickett's Charge at Gettysburg (July 3, 1863) ended with at least 1,125 Confederate attackers killed and 4,550 wounded; on a broad field at Cold Harbor, Virginia (June 1864), 7,000 advancing Union soldiers were killed or wounded. And none of these attacks accomplished anything more than to demonstrate that Napoleon's tactics didn't work anymore.

The range and accuracy of the rifled musket had similar effects on cavalry and artillery units, pushing them back from the front line so they were out of rifled-musket range.

In almost every way, the rifled musket shifted the advantage from the attacker to the defender. It was a lesson that the commanders on both sides were tragically slow to learn.

Muzzleloaded rifled muskets unquestionably caused the largest number of wounds and deaths in Civil War battles. But as accurate and effective as rifled muzzleloaders were, they took a long time to load, and the soldier usually had to stand up to reload, exposing himself to enemy fire.

The next advance eliminated many of these problems. It was the breech-loaded rifle. Breech-loading meant that the bullet was inserted, not from the muzzle, but from the opposite end of the barrel: the breech. To load each round, the breech end had to be opened and then sealed up again before the next shot. Otherwise, the force of the explosion would blast out in the shooter's face instead of going down the gun barrel.

There had been breech-loading guns before the Civil War. Christian Sharps was selling a breech-loading sporting rifle, the first version of his breechloader, by 1850. However, no breechloader was in common use by either army at the start of the war.

The Confederates suffered heavy losses on Cemetery Hill at Gettysburg.
Longer-range rifled muskets often made frontal charges almost suicidal.

Later versions of the Sharps rifle, with various improvements, were among the first breechloaders to be used in the war. The Sharps carbine (a short-barreled rifle for use on horseback or in tight quarters) was especially popular with cavalry units.

The Sharps guns used a cartridge with a paper or linen outer casing that was wrapped around the base of a bullet, with the nose of the bullet exposed (*see page 93*). The cylinder formed by the outer casing was filled with gunpowder and sealed at the base. The cartridge could be loaded as a

unit into the breech. The breech lock sliced off the base of the cartridge as the lock closed, exposing the gunpowder inside so it was ready to be ignited.

All the shooter of the Sharps had to do was open the breech, put in the cartridge, close the breech, put on a fresh percussion cap, and fire. He could load the gun when he was crouched over, lying down, or on horseback. As a bonus, a breech-loading bullet could be made to fit more tightly into the barrel than was practical with a muzzle-loading bullet. This made for a better gas seal and allowed the bullet to travel farther and straighter when fired.

Good as the Sharps was, its paper or linen cartridges were easily damaged and absorbed moisture. And fumbling with a percussion cap still slowed down loading.

Gun designers soon hit upon the idea of all-metal cartridges with built-in percussion caps on the base. This was the forerunner to the modern cartridge bullet. Its basic features were the same as those of bullets in use today. They were more durable, more resistant to dust and moisture, and far easier to handle than any previous cartridges.

The Spencer repeating rifle that Lincoln fired that August day in 1863 took the next logical step: loading multiple rounds. Seven all-metal cartridges could be loaded into the weapon at once by sliding a metal tube loaded with cartridges into the gunstock (*see above*). A spring mechanism pushed the cartridges forward. Pulling a lever down ejected the old cartridge. Pulling it up drew a fresh round up and into the firing mechanism and sealed the breech for firing.

Pull the lever down, cock the hammer, aim the rifle, and pull the trigger. It took longer to say it than to do it. A Spencer repeating rifle had a firing rate of 14 shots a minute. As its limited but effective use during the Gettysburg campaign proved, this revolution in firepower gave Union troops a deadly and decisive advantage.

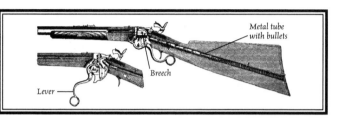

The Spencer Repeating Rifle held seven cartridges in the gunstock. Pulling a lever ejected the spent cartridge and loaded a fresh one.

But that would only matter if far more such rifles were manufactured and issued to the troops.

Artillery officers were also discovering that rifled cannon, like their smaller cousins, shot farther, more accurately, and with far more power than smoothbore cannon. More and more rifled guns rolled out of both Union and Confederate arsenals. Experiments with breech-loaded cannon were moving forward, but they were not perfected in time to be of use in the war.

Other new weapons were under development. One of the most important was the Union repeating gun, an ancestor of the machine gun. The first version was named the "coffee-mill gun" by President Lincoln because it resembled a kitchen gadget for grinding coffee beans. Supposedly it could fire 120 rounds of ammunition a minute. Various other types of rapid-fire repeating guns were also demonstrated during the war, and a few,

The "coffee-mill gun" fired lots of bullets quickly but proved unreliable under battle conditions.

including the coffee-mill gun, saw limited service. Such guns could fire a lot of bullets quickly, but they were as big and unwieldy as small cannon and not much easier to aim. They were ungainly contraptions liable to break down at any time, and it seemed no one could quite decide whether they were a form of artillery or a new kind of infantry weapon. Not until World War I would effective tactics be developed for machine guns.

Inventing a new weapon was by no means the same as perfecting it and making it reliable and useful enough for the army to use—and figuring out how best to use it. A small number of revolutionary weapons like the Spencer were made ready for service during the war, thanks in large part to the Commander in Chief, but the expected wholesale revolution in warfare did not follow.

Much of the reason for that could be traced to one man:

Chief of Army Ordnance Colonel James W. Ripley. Early in the war he wrote that a "great evil now specially prevalent…is the vast variety of the new inventions, each having, of course, its advocates.…The influence thus exercised has already introduced into the service many kinds and calibers of arms." They were "unfit for use as military weapons," he said, and none was as good as the American rifled, muzzleloading musket.

This great variety of weapons was, according to Ripley, "producing confusion in the manufacture, the issue, and the use of ammunition, and very injurious to the efficiency of troops. This evil can only be stopped by positively refusing to answer any requisitions for or propositions to sell new and untried arms, and steadily adhering to the rule of uniformity of arms for all troops.…"

Ripley, who had great influence over the selection and

purchase of weapons, wanted to place a total ban on all new inventions. He might as well have put up a sign reading "No Better Ideas."

It is easy to make fun of Ripley's opinions today. But his policy was not as silly as it seemed. Ripley set down his rule at the beginning of the war, when many believed that it would all be ended quickly by one big battle.

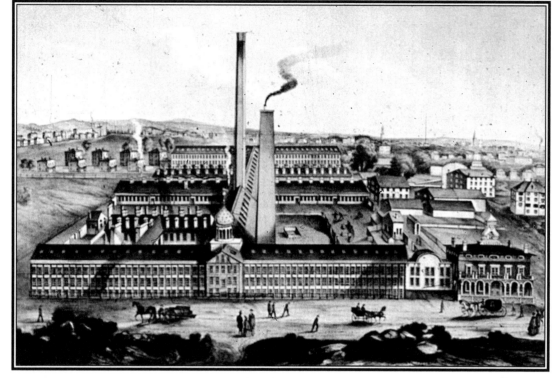

One of the most powerful Northern weapons was the factory, such as Samuel Colt's in Connecticut. Widespread mass production gave the Union a huge advantage over the shortage-plagued South.

It took a lot of time and money to set up a factory and start producing a new kind of weapon. If Ripley had placed orders for a half dozen types of rifles and ordered ten thousand of each, some or all of the new gun types might have turned out to have hidden flaws. And what if the war had been short and all the guns were delivered on schedule—after the fighting was over?

Even if the war were still raging and even if all half-dozen different kinds of guns did work as promised, Ripley would have had to supply six different kinds of ammunition and keep track of which unit was using what gun. There would have to be six different sets of weapons manuals, repair depots, spare parts, weapons trainers, and on and on. Standardization, the basis of his policy, made sense. Besides, he already had a problem. At one point, the Union army's artillery service kept more than 600 different kinds of ammunition in stock. It was considered an accomplishment to get that number down to a mere 140!

Ripley was also fending off a constant parade of inventors and agents for inventors. Many, like Spencer and ironclad designer Ericsson, managed to get President Lincoln interested in their inventions. Lincoln, by observing or participating in at least 30 tests or demonstrations of rifles, cannon, shells, explosives, and other military hardware during the war, added to Ripley's labors by forcing him to evaluate the merit of many innovations. Senators, Congressmen, Cabinet members, and influential mayors and editors—plus the friends and relations of all of those men—were each, as Ripley put it, "insisting on the superiority of his favorite arm over all others and urging its adoption by the Government."

A new weapon had to be reliable, affordable, and easy for the troops to use without a great deal of training. It had to be manufactured in large enough quantities at a low enough price, as did its ammunition and parts. And it had to be so much better than what the army already had that it was worth the time, expense, risk, and disruption of introducing it into service.

That standard of performance was, perhaps, much higher than Lincoln realized at first. But he learned quickly. As time went by, he supported and pushed for the development of fewer and fewer of the new and wondrous weapons and gadgets that were brought to his attention.

But the Spencer repeating rifle clearly exceeded even that high standard. Lincoln had arranged, over Ripley's objections, for 10,000 of them to be ordered at the end of 1861. However, the new weapon had faced exactly the sort of delays that Ripley feared. The first guns were not delivered until almost a year later. The first Sharps rifles and carbines went into battle in 1862. However, there were only about 2,000 of them, and they were distributed to small, specialized units. Still they produced glowing reports from the Union forces that used them.

The new weapons had another, more subtle advantage. The Confederate army routinely armed itself mainly with captured Union weapons. That worked well enough for guns but not for ammunition. The Confederacy in large part made its own bullets to go into the captured Northern guns. But Spencer cartridges were much more complicated than Minié balls, and the South simply was not able to manufacture them. Any Spencers captured by the South would be rendered useless as soon as the cartridges grabbed with them were used up. And, of course, there wasn't any hope of the Confederacy mass-producing its own repeaters.

Ripley, still opposed to the Sharps and the Spencer, grudgingly allowed cavalry forces to use Spencer carbines, but continued to resist giving repeating rifles to regular infantry troops, in part because he felt that providing soldiers with a gun that shot faster would merely result in using up more ammunition.

One anonymous soldier responded to that criticism, inviting those who said soldiers with rapid-fire guns would waste ammunition to imagine themselves going "to the front armed with one Springfield musket, and oppose themselves to an equal number of Rebs armed with repeaters or breech-loaders....[and] offer themselves as a target to some fellow on the other side who has nothing to do but cock his piece and blaze away."

When Mr. Lincoln raised that Spencer rifle to his shoulder, the Battle of Gettysburg was only six weeks in the past. In repeated encounters before, during, and after the great battle, whenever the Confederates were facing a small unit armed with repeaters or even single-shot breechloaders, they came away believing that they were facing a much larger force, because a small group of men suddenly had the firepower of a larger unit.

Men in those small units had more firepower, could reload more quickly, and could do so without having to stand up while reloading. Even if that smaller unit used more ammunition per man, it used up far less of everything else—food, shoes, horses, uniforms, tents— than did larger units using old-style weapons.

The superior firepower provided by repeaters might have been enough to win a battle or even enough to end the war. But Ripley did not see it that way. As a result, large-scale

This advanced, high-powered, wrought-iron cannon was the most expensive gun built for the war. The fighting was over before it was ready for service.

distribution of breechloaders and repeaters would have to wait until he was forced to retire, less than a month after Lincoln and Spencer had their target practice. Increasing the production of these weapons and ammunitions still took time. And getting the new rifles to the troops was a slow process that only began to make real headway as the war was coming to a close.

More and more Union soldiers were issued breechloaders and repeaters in 1864 and 1865, and the Confederate soldiers rapidly learned to dread coming up against them. "I think the Johnnys are getting rattled; they are afraid of our repeating rifles," a Union soldier wrote. "They say we are not fair, that we have guns that we load up on Sunday and shoot all the rest of the week."

No one could any longer doubt the superiority of the rapid-fire, breech-loading, repeating rifle. Even so, in the last battles of the war, most soldiers on both sides were still standing up to load their weapons from the muzzle end—the same way their great-grandfathers had in the Revolutionary War.

Although the Confederacy could not match the development of high-power Union weapons encouraged by Lincoln, a few daring Southern patriots were preparing to risk their lives in a terrifying secret weapon: the submarine.

The *U.S.S.* Hartford *fights its way past Rebel warships, including the ironclad C.S.S.* Manassas *(far right), between Fort Jackson and Fort St. Philip on the Mississippi River. This April 1862 action led to the capture of New Orleans, denying the Confederacy a vital port.*

CHAPTER TEN

· THE HOMEMADE NAVY ·

On August 29, 1863, an inexperienced Confederate naval officer boarded a remarkable new vessel, determined to attack the enemy. The vessel was the submarine *H.L. Hunley*, and she was about to kill half her crew. It would not be the last—or worst—disaster to befall her. Nor was it the first or last desperate Confederate attempt to use advanced technology to push back the overwhelming power of the Union navy.

The story of the *H.L. Hunley* is almost pure tragedy. It begins in New Orleans, where James R. McClintock, Baxter Watson, and Horace Lawson Hunley built their first submarine, the *Pioneer*. When Union forces took New Orleans in April 1862, the three inventors departed for Mobile, Alabama. There they joined forces with Thomas Park and Thomas Lyons and built a second sub, the unsuccessful *American Diver*. The inventors kept on

The Hunley *was too small to stand up in.*

trying, with Horace Hunley providing the bulk of the financial support. For that reason, the third boat was named after him, though one source says the naming took place later—in memorium—after the boat had killed him. The team demonstrated the *Hunley* for Franklin Buchanan, the first commander of the C.S.S. *Virginia*. At the time, he was commander of Mobile's naval defenses.

The *Hunley* was just under 40 feet long, less than 4 feet wide, and 4 feet, 3 inches from top to bottom. Eight or 9 men were crammed into that space, all but one sitting sideways on a bench. She was propelled by means of a gigantic crank that ran the length of the tiny vessel. The crank was attached to the propeller. The men on the bench used their muscle power to turn the crank and move the craft along, while the captain steered from the forward position.

The *Hunley* was sometimes referred to as the C.S.S. *Hunley*, but she was privately built and never formally purchased by or commissioned into the Confederate navy. She was designed to attack by using a torpedo, which today would be called a bomb or a mine, placed on the end of a 17-foot iron pole, or spar, on the bow of the boat. A barbed metal point was fixed to the front of the torpedo. The plan was for the *Hunley* to ram the torpedo deep into the wooden hull of the ship being attacked, then back away. The torpedo, which was connected by a line to the *Hunley*, was designed to stay jammed into the enemy hull. A pull on the line after the *Hunley* was at a safe distance would detonate the explosive charge and blow up the enemy ship.

Transported by two railroad flat cars attached together, the *Hunley* rode the rails to Charleston, South Carolina,

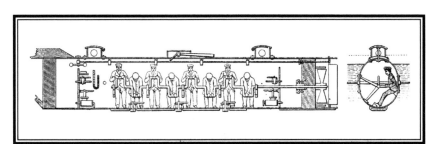

Eight men turned a giant crank running the length of the Hunley *in order to turn her screw and move her through the water.*

arriving on August 12, 1863. She went right to work trying to get close enough to Union ships blockading the harbor to sink them. But after two weeks, her civilian crew had failed to accomplish anything. Impatient for results, Confederate Lieutenant John Payne took command. He was at the controls on August 29 when, somehow, the *Hunley* went to the bottom. Payne and three of the crew escaped, but five others drowned.

The boat was recovered, and the dead bodies were removed. Horace Hunley was determined to try again. On October 15, Hunley himself was in command of a training mission, during which he failed to close a flood valve. The boat sank, killing all eight aboard.

She was raised once again, the bodies were removed again, and Lieutenant George E. Dixon took command. He spent months training his men thoroughly. By year's end

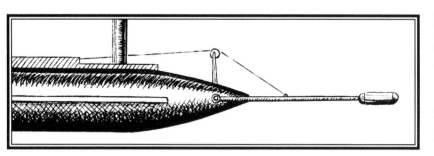

The Hunley's only weapon was a spar torpedo (a bomb on a pole) similar to the one attached to the bow of this experimental Confederate attack boat.

they were ready, but most of the blockade ships were anchored too far away for the hand-cranked *Hunley* to reach them through the choppy waters of winter seas. Finally, on February 17, 1864, the U.S.S. *Housatonic* dropped anchor a mere four miles from shore.

The officer of the watch aboard the *Housatonic* saw what looked like a plank of wood moving through the water toward the ship. He raised the alarm. Several shots were fired at the *Hunley* while an attempt was made to get the *Housatonic* moving, but it was too late. A terrific explosion tore off the *Housatonic*'s stern. She went beneath the waves, along with five of her crew.

Those watching on shore later reported seeing a blue light on the water, the "mission accomplished" signal from the *Hunley*. But then no more was seen or heard of

her. It is still not known exactly how or why she sank.

The *Hunley* was the first operational Confederate submarine— and the last. She had succeeded in destroying an enemy ship, the first submarine in history to do so. But during the course of her career, she killed 25 Confederates and only 5 of the enemy. Sinking that one ship came at the cost of her own destruction, years of effort, and great expense. The attack on the *Housatonic* was a victory, but as was too often true, one that left the Confederacy weaker than before.

Stephen Mallory, Confederate Secretary of the Navy, had to gamble that technology could buy other victories. Mallory knew he could never build a naval force anywhere near as large as the wartime Union navy. He therefore decided to build a more advanced navy. "Inequality of numbers may be compensated by invulnerability," he wrote.

"Not only does economy, but naval success, dictate the wisdom and expediency of fighting with iron against wood, without regard to first cost."

The effort to build ironclads at home put him face to face with all the challenges of confronting Northern technological and industrial power. Northern ironclads were mass-produced in large shipyards by experienced shipbuilders using specialized equipment. The Southern ships had to be made by hand in ones and twos.

Mallory tried to get ironclads built in Britain and France, seeking "ships that can receive without material injury the fire of the heaviest frigates and liners at short distance and whose guns, though few in number…will enable them to destroy the wooden navy of our enemy." But Union diplomats succeeded in stopping construction on two ships in England. One ship was built in France but did not reach American waters until the war was over.

Twenty or so Confederate ironclads were eventually built. Some—notably the C.S.S. *Albemarle* and the C.S.S. *Arkansas*—were successful in many ways, but most of them were underpowered, hard to maneuver, and noted for their infuriating mechanical failures. Like the C.S.S. *Virginia*, they were often built from scrounged materials, using surplus, worn-out engines that had been made for some other purpose. Instead of being used for aggressive attacks, they served mainly in defensive roles, protecting the dwindling number of Confederate ports that were still open. However, they were very effective in that role. Just knowing an ironclad was nearby was often enough to keep wooden-hulled Union blockade ships from venturing too close.

The last major confrontation between the homemade Confederate ironclad navy and the Union blockade fleet came on August 5, 1864, when the ironclad C.S.S. *Tennessee* sailed out into Mobile Bay, Alabama. In command was Franklin Buchanan.

The *Tennessee*'s engine, salvaged from a river steamboat, wasn't big enough for the vessel, and the ship had other major technical flaws, but she was the most powerful Confederate ship on the scene. She led three unarmored gunboats into battle against a Union flotilla of wooden ships and four ironclads determined to close the last

The defeat of the C.S.S. Tennessee *in the Battle of Mobile Bay closed the last Confederate port on the Gulf Coast, hastening the end of the war.*

open port on the Confederacy's Gulf Coast. The Northern ships soon chased the small gunboats away, leaving the *Tennessee* to face the Union fleet alone.

One Northern iron-clad struck a mine and sank, breaking up the Union formation. The *Tennessee* kept firing, severely damaging another Union ship. Two others rammed her again and again, suffering more damage than they inflicted. The Northern ships surrounded the *Tennessee* and kept up a relentless rate of fire, wrecking her steering and knocking out her steam plant.

She could no longer turn or move, but she kept firing until Union guns shot off the chains that held one of her gun ports open, jamming it shut. But it was only when her iron shield was on the point of collapse that the wounded Buchanan allowed her to surrender.

The *Tennessee* was underpowered, built under impossible conditions with a salvaged engine, manned by inexperienced sailors, outnumbered, and outgunned. Still she fought bravely against a better-armed, better-trained foe until her flaws caught up with her captain's aggressive, perhaps even foolhardy, courage.

Mallory's ironclads proved to be another example of how the Confederacy wound up spending vast amounts of money, time, and materials on projects that failed to accomplish the miracles the South needed. The sea blockade was growing tighter. The Confederacy's homemade iron ships could not break it. But iron rails had already broken a land blockade—the siege of Chattanooga.

A cannon-carrying armored railcar manned by Union soldiers protects workers repairing a bridge burned by Southern sympathizers in Maryland. The Union railroad network was far superior to the Confederacy's system.

CHAPTER ELEVEN

· RAILS & WIRES AT WAR ·

✠

Even when the war was well into its third year, some Union generals, including then General in Chief Henry W. Halleck, did not share their Commander in Chief's faith in the ability of railroads to change the course of a battle or save an army under siege. The dramatic events of September 1863 would force the generals to change their minds.

Union Major General William S. Rosecrans had taken Chattanooga, Tennessee, a key rail center, with some of his troops. He sent the rest in pursuit of the Confederates. The Southerners withdrew into northwestern Georgia to await reinforcements coming from Mississippi and Virginia. Because much of the South's railway system was by then either in Union hands or in shambles, the Virginia reinforcements had a long and maddening journey full of delays caused by wrecked bridges and mismatched equipment.

A telegraph operator sends an urgent message.

The pursued Confederates at first evaded Rosecrans's men by maneuvering northward through mountain gaps and along ridges. Then the armies clashed in a fierce battle along Chickamauga Creek, 12 miles south of Chattanooga. Both sides lost many men as the Confederates doggedly drove through the Union line, forcing Rosecrans's troops back to Chattanooga. About 40,000 Confederates laid siege to the city, holding road and railway routes and blocking the Tennessee River to Union ships.

Curious to know what kind of job Rosecrans was doing, Lincoln had sent Assistant Secretary of War Charles Dana, a former journalist, to Tennessee to provide him with an eyewitness account of his major general in battle. On September 20 Dana telegraphed Lincoln details of the Chickamauga defeat. In a separate telegram to the War Department, Rosecrans said that he did not know whether

Besieged in Chattanooga, Union soldiers tore down houses for shelter, firewood, and a wallpapered stockade. Railroads will save them.

he could hold Chattanooga. Lincoln responded by promising that some way would be found to help him.

On September 22, having no news from Rosecrans, Lincoln telegraphed him again, asking what was happening. Rosecrans said he still held the city with 30,000 men but that he could only pray they would survive. Lincoln tried to encourage Rosecrans, but the President told an aide that Rosecrans was "stunned and confused, like a duck hit on the head."

Just before midnight on September 23, Lincoln, Secretary of War Stanton, General in Chief Halleck, and others met in a council of war to plan a way to save the 30,000 besieged soldiers. Stanton estimated that Rosecrans and his men could hold out for 10 days—long enough for 30,000 more men from the Army of the Potomac to reach and rescue them. Halleck was shocked. Such a massive military operation, he said, would take 40 days.

Not 40, Stanton said, 5—by train. They would travel from Virginia, across the Appalachian Mountains, then south through Kentucky into Tennessee. Even Lincoln, disappointed so often by his generals, said, "I will bet that if an order is given tonight, the troops could not be got to Washington in five days."

When the war began, Lincoln had seen both the railroad and the telegraph as military tools. When Lincoln wanted a new general after the disastrous Union defeat at Bull Run in July 1861, he selected George B. McClellan—a man who knew more about the telegraph and railroads than any other general in the North or South.

McClellan disappointed Lincoln as a commander, but the President still made use of his expertise on railroad matters. Eight days after McClellan was put in command of

Union troops around Washington, he sent a memorandum to Lincoln, noting that because railroads had "introduced a new and very important element into the war," they should come under government control. Lincoln successfully urged Congress to pass a law giving the President power to "take possession of any or all" railroads and telegraph lines in the United States.

Rather than submit to a government takeover, railroad officials in the North quickly agreed to cooperate with the army, carrying soldiers and military freight at strictly enforced low rates. In the South, the new law gave the Union control over rail lines wherever the Union army seized territory. The United States Military Railroad (U.S.M.R.R.) eventually ran 2,105 miles of tracks in occupied areas of the Confederacy.

Even before the war, the South had lagged behind the North not only in railroad-track mileage but also in the number of factories for making locomotives and railcars. At the beginning of the war, the South had 8,783 miles of track compared to the Union's 22,385 miles. The South's railroads were owned by hundreds of companies. Most Southern railroads were short-haul lines, used for jobs such as transporting cotton to a river port or steamboat landing.

Because the Confederate Congress supported state control over federal control, it took two years to pass a law allowing the Confederacy to force railroads to handle military traffic speedily and at fair cost. Even with such a law passed, Confederate officials had trouble controlling their railroads. But as disorganized as the Confederacy's railroads were, they often did manage to move troops when and where they were needed—as they had at Manassas during the First Battle of Bull Run.

As soon as the U.S.M.R.R. was created in 1862, it took control of seven miles of track that the War Department had laid near Washington, crossing the Potomac River by way of Long Bridge and entering Union-occupied Virginia. As men of the U.S.M.R.R. Construction Corps began to extend tracks deeper into Virginia, they came up against a problem that plagued railroads of both North and South: the tracks did not fit together.

If you looked at a map of railroads at the beginning of the war, you would think that the North had such a network of rails that, east of the Mississippi River, trains could travel almost anywhere. But what the map would not show you is that the tracks were so different that trains could not easily pass from one place to another. The problem was track gauge, the width between the parallel rails of tracks.

In most of New England and in Indiana and Illinois, for example, the width between rails was 4 feet, 8 $\frac{1}{2}$ inches. In Ohio, the width was 4 feet, 10 inches. These were only two of the several different track widths that slowed down the movement of passengers and freight. When a train had to pass from the tracks of one width, or gauge, to the tracks of another gauge, the train usually had to stop and transfer whatever it was carrying to another train with wheels that would fit on the next set of rails. Some railroads got around this problem by slipping an additional rail into the track bed so that two widths could be used. Or a train might have wheels that could be adjusted to different widths. But all these were awkward makeshifts, not full solutions. No matter how a train solved the problem, the varying track gauges produced delays.

Deciding that 4 feet, 8 $\frac{1}{2}$ inches would be the "standard

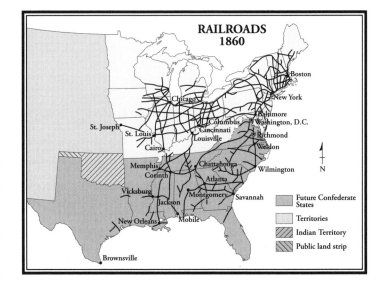

Prewar, the North had a far denser network of railroad lines than the states that would form the Confederacy.

gauge," the U.S.M.R.R. began laying track of that width and ordering locomotives and cars with wheels to fit that gauge. That meant Union troops and supplies could move smoothly and swiftly along every track built by or for the U.S.M.R.R. The orders produced a manufacturing boom in the North and laid the foundation for a standard-gauge railroad system throughout the country.

Just as important as building the rails was maintaining them—particularly in the face of very determined Rebel raiders and saboteurs, agents who destroy enemy property.

A Union worker uses a special tool to straighten track. Rebels heated torn-up rails in the middle then bent them around trees.

Early in the war, Southern forces in Virginia wrecked a bridge to slow down Union forces. Herman Haupt, a skilled railroad builder who ran the U.S.M.R.R. in the area of Washington, set to work with untrained labor drawn from army ranks. His men cut two million feet of timber and replaced the bridge with amazing speed (*see back cover*). The President himself went to take a look at it and even walked across it. He reported that he had "seen the most remarkable structure that human eyes ever rested upon. That man Haupt has built a bridge across Potomac Creek, about 400 feet long and nearly 100 feet high, over which loaded trains are running every hour, and, upon my word, gentlemen, there is nothing in it but beanpoles and cornstalks."

Later in the war trained rail repair teams were regarded as being an essential arm of the service. The repair teams were so good that one Confederate railroad wrecker supposedly complained that it was no use destroying a rail tunnel "'cause [Union Major General] Sherman carries 'long duplicates of all the tunnels!"

The establishment of an organized, standardized rail system was a large part of what made the plan to break the siege of Chattanooga possible.

Also in the room during the planning conference for the great troop movement to rescue Rosecrans's troops was Brigadier General Daniel C. McCallum, former general superintendent of the Erie Railroad and the current director and superintendent of the U.S.M.R.R. Lincoln and Stanton turned to him. He scribbled some figures on a

*Members of the Union Army Signal Corps string up telegraph wires
during the Battle of Fredericksburg, linking the battlefield to Washington.*

piece of paper and said that he could get 20,000 men to Chattanooga in 7 days. Lincoln backed the plan, and the complex maneuver began.

Telegrams went out to alert the railroads and the Army of the Potomac. Within 9 days rails carried some 20,000 men, along with 3,000 horses and mules, to the vicinity of Chattanooga in eastern Tennessee. From Mississippi via boat, rail, and hard march came another 17,000 men.

Major General Ulysses S. Grant, to whom Lincoln had just given command of Union forces in the West, personally led the campaign to break the siege of Chattanooga. In a few months, Lincoln would promote Grant to lieutenant general and make him General in Chief of the Union army, replacing Halleck, whose 40-day prediction about ending the siege had helped to end his career.

With sufficient troops, supplies, and equipment at hand, Grant and his subordinates drove the Confederate forces away from Chattanooga in a series of engagements. Troops under Major Generals William Tecumseh Sherman and Joseph Hooker enveloped the Confederate flanks.

· ARMY FOOD ·

When Ulysses S. Grant broke the six-week siege of Chattanooga in 1863, his immediate concern was the thousands of hungry Union troops in the city. "They had been so long on short rations," he later wrote, "that my first thought was the establishment of a line over which food might reach them." He had reached Chattanooga on a 60-mile supply route through knee-deep mud on a steep, twisting road.

Grant's forces fought a desperate battle to seize a riverside site from which they could establish a shorter, better land-water supply line. On October 30th, the first steamboat, coincidentally named *Chattanooga*, brought in tons of food and supplies. The hungry troops greeted the ship with the cry, "The Cracker Line is open. Full rations, boys!"

Union soldiers called the route The Cracker Line after a kind of cracker known as hardtack, which was made from flour and water. Soldiers sometimes made "skillygalee"— hardtack soaked in water and fried in pork fat until brown.

Union soldiers' diets also included food brought to them in tin cans. The canning of food had been going on for a while, but the war spurred the development of the idea that meals could travel. New processing techniques kept canned milk, meat, and vegetables from spoiling on their way from canning plants to soldiers' stomachs. Many Northerners had their first taste of food out of a can as Union soldiers. (Rebel troops didn't have much canned or processed food.) When the war ended, they carried home a demand for food in a can. By 1870 canneries were producing 30 million cans of food a year compared to about 5 million when the war started.

Hooker's forces won at Lookout Mountain. Sherman's forces moved on Tunnel Hill with less success. Then Major General George H. Thomas's men charged up Missionary Ridge. Ordered to advance on the first of three lines of defense, they routed the Confederates, chasing them clear up and over the crest of the ridge. The victory was so complete it surprised even the Union soldiers. The Rebel armies retreated into Georgia, never to return.

The victory at Chattanooga did more than spotlight the military importance of railroads. The telegraph also played a vital role in making the rescue happen. And many of the telegrams were sent on their way by President Lincoln.

By making the War Department's telegraph office his military nerve center, Lincoln became a Commander in Chief unlike any President before him. Day by day, night by night, battle by battle, he read countless telegraph messages and sent out a steady stream of his own.

Although devices for printing telegrams had been invented, military telegrams were almost always handwritten. An operator sent a message by using a telegraph key to produce a series of dots and dashes (such as dot-dash

· MORSE CODE ·

Samuel F.B. Morse

Fascinated by the properties of electricity after hearing a lecture at Yale, Samuel Morse had an idea that eventually led to the telegraph. But, he did not know much about electricity, so he got some help from a professor of chemistry who had read an 1831 article by Joseph Henry of Princeton. Henry had used an electromagnet to ring a bell hooked up to an electric circuit. Henry later became the first Secretary of the Smithsonian Institution and friend of Abraham Lincoln.

Morse responded to the offer of a federal government reward by developing a system for sending messages by a code that now bears his name. Morse code transformed the alphabet into dots and dashes. He built a 40-mile electric line strung on poles and trees from Washington to Baltimore. Then on May 24, 1844, he sent a message—WHAT HATH GOD WROUGHT?—that won him not only $30,000 from Congress but also global fame. Although Morse got the credit for a successful communication system, it was Henry's earlier work that laid the foundation for the telegraph.

for the letter *a*) called Morse code. The receiving operator listened to the stream of dots and dashes coming from the telegraph "sounder" and then wrote down the message, letter by letter, in longhand.

Some generals did not like the way Lincoln peppered them with questions about the "news" he had picked up from War Department telegrams and other sources. THE RECENT MOVEMENT OF YOUR ARMY IS ENDED WITHOUT EFFECTING ITS OBJECT, he once telegraphed a general. WHAT NEXT? HAVE YOU ALREADY IN YOUR MIND A PLAN WHOLLY, OR PARTIALLY FORMED? IF YOU HAVE, PROSECUTE IT WITHOUT INTERFERENCE FROM ME. IF YOU HAVE NOT, PLEASE INFORM ME, SO THAT I, INCOMPETENT AS I MAY BE, CAN TRY [to] ASSIST IN THE FORMATION OF SOME PLAN FOR THE ARMY. His messages were signed A. LINCOLN and could not be ignored.

Important messages were sent in code. To encode a message, a telegraph operator began by selecting a "keyword" card, which was like a little code book with its own keyword label. Each card had different instructions about how a message was to be scrambled. It might order setting up a grid of 7 columns on 11 lines with a route for the message: first word at the bottom of the 6th column, second word at the top of the 3rd column, and so forth. The card also contained a list of what operators called "arbitraries," meaning randomly selected code names for certain people, places, and military phrases. Prominent people, such as

Lincoln and generals, would have several arbitraries so that the same word would not keep repeating. By substituting an arbitrary for a real word or phrase, the operator made the message tougher for code breakers.

To decipher the message, the receiving operator would look at his set of keyword cards, pick out the one used by the message sender, and then use the same system to unscramble the message. The text of such a scrambled message would read something like this:

WASHINGTON, D. C., JULY 15, 1863.

A. H. CALDWELL, CIPHER-OPERATOR,

GEN. MEADE'S HEADQUARTERS:

BLONDE BLESS OF WHO NO OPTIC TO GET AN IMPRESSION I MADISON SQUARE BROWN CAMMER TOBY AX THE HAVE TURNIP ME HARRY BITCH RUSTLE SILK ADRIAN COUNSEL LOCUST YOU ANOTHER ONLY OF CHILDREN SERENADE FLEA KNOX COUNTY FOR WOOD THAT AWL TIES GET HOUND WHO WAS WAR HIM SUICIDE ON FOR WAS PLEASE VILLAGE LARGE BAT BUNYAN GIVE SIGH INCUBUS HEAVY NORRIS ON TRAMMELED CAT KNIT STRIVEN WITHOUT IF MADRID QUAIL UPRIGHT MARTYR STEWART MAN MUCH BEAR SINCE ASS SKELETON TELL THE OPPRESSING TYLER MONKEY.

BATES.

The first word was always the keyword. In this example, the word "Blonde" directed the receiving operator to the correct keyword card. When unscrambled, the message could be read across, line by line (with some "padding," or false words, added by the operator, such as "bless him" in the message below, to further confuse a code breaker). Here is the scrambled message unscrambled:

Washington, D.C.	July	15th	18	60	3	for
Sigh	man	Cammer	on	period	I	would
give	much	to be	relieved	of the	impression	that
Meade	comma	Couch	comma	Smith	and	all
comma	since	the	battle	of	get	ties
burg	Comma	have	striven	only	to	get
the enemy	over	the river	without	another	fight	period
please	tell	me	if	you	know	who
was	the	one	corps	commander	who	was
for	fighting	comma	in the	council	of	war
on	Sunday	might	signature	A. Lincoln	Bless	him

Telegraphers on both sides learned how to tap the telegraph lines of the enemy. A tapper in a remote spot along the line climbed a pole carrying two parallel, insulated wires, scraped off the India-rubber insulation (an elastic, gummy substance from the sap of "rubber" trees), and

Inner and outer wheels of Confederate cipher wheels lined up enciphered and deciphered letters in secret messages.

wrapped the exposed wires with his own wires, to which he attached his own telegraph key. He could then listen to the dots and dashes and write down the message.

A tapper could read uncoded messages, but all the important messages were in code. Baffled Confederates sometimes had Southern newspapers publish intercepted coded messages in the hope that a reader could break the code. Union telegraphers boasted that none of their coded messages was ever broken.

Messages sent by the Confederate army were frequently cracked by Union code breakers, who sometimes used their knowledge to send the Southerners false intelligence in coded messages that appeared to come from a Confederate operator. The Confederates used a simpler cipher system, substituting a message's letters with other letters or symbols. Lincoln often hovered over Union code breakers, fascinated by seeing an unreadable message become readable.

The Confederacy made far less use of telegraphy than the Union did. Telegraph operators were few in the South when the war began. A survey made in 1857 showed that Northern states had 1,467 telegraph stations while the states that would form the Confederacy had only 107. The South did find more operators during the war, but the Confederacy never did come close to matching the U.S. Military Telegraph Service.

Despite its name, the telegraph service was not part of the army. It was a civilian organization run directly by Lincoln's administration. Generals might not have liked that, but he was the Commander in Chief, and they had to obey his orders. Although the operators were civilians, they accompanied units into battle, risking their lives alongside soldiers. More than 300 operators were killed in action, died from disease or wounds, or suffered in prisoner of war camps.

Although the operations of the telegraph office settled

· MEDICINE ·

The age of invention and discovery did not mean much to soldiers wounded or suffering from disease. Not until after the war did the use of anesthetics become routine. And only then came an understanding of the importance of cleanliness, sterilization, and other methods to curb infection—even the rule that a surgeon should wash his hands before operating.

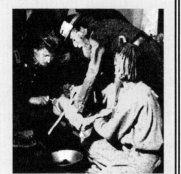

A Union doctor shows how to perform an amputation.

Throughout the war, far more soldiers died of disease or wound infections than from gunshots. Accurate figures are not known, but here are the estimates. Union battle deaths: 110,070; death from disease and wounds: 250,150. Confederate battle deaths: 94,000; from disease and wounds: 164,000.

Mostly because of bad sanitation and other poor public health practices, communicable diseases swept through army and prisoner of war camps.

Large percentages of military units often were too sick to fight. The U.S. Sanitary Commission did make major improvements in Union camp sanitation, which, in turn, significantly improved soldiers' health. The main job of army surgeons on both sides was to amputate severely wounded limbs. They amputated to save the soldier's life, because a badly damaged limb could become infected, spreading deadly bacteria into the body.

down to a smoother professionalism in the later stages of the war, things did not proceed as well in the war's earlier days. As was often the case, McClellan had something to do with the difficulties.

Even though McClellan had suggested that Lincoln take control of the telegraph, he highly disapproved of the Commander in Chief's use of the telegraph to keep track of his generals. McClellan, being a vain man, resented taking orders from Lincoln.

McClellan ordered that a separate telegraph wire be strung to his headquarters in a building near the War Department and further ordered that he, as commanding general in Washington, was to be the first person to receive all messages about military activities around the capital.

Lincoln now had another telegraph office to visit. One day, when a message containing bad news came in, McClellan's aide slipped it under the blotter on his desk. Lincoln learned of the hidden dispatch and asked the aide why he had kept it from his Commander in Chief. The embarrassed aide told of McClellan's show-to-me-first order. Lincoln did not confront McClellan about the order. But

A Union telegraph line goes up alongside a Southern railway during Major General William Tecumseh Sherman's Atlanta campaign.

many times after that day, when Lincoln walked into McClellan's headquarters and asked for the latest messages, he smiled and asked the aide, "Is there not something under the blotter?" Secretary of War Edwin M. Stanton later ordered that all telegrams go directly to the War Department's telegraph office, which Lincoln so frequently visited.

As the war ground on, other generals had difficulties adjusting to the way the telegraph and the railroad were changing war. Even Sherman, who was a brilliant strategist, had a prejudice against railroads in warfare. He once said he was "much obliged" to the Tennessee River as a dependable transportation route, "for I am never easy with a railroad which takes a whole army to guard, each foot of rail being essential to the whole; whereas, they [the Rebels] can't stop the Tennessee [River], and each boat can make its own game."

Yet Sherman's Atlanta campaign depended upon railroads. On July 12, 1864, Sherman telegraphed Grant: MY RAILROAD AND TELEGRAPH ARE NOW UP AND WE ARE RAPIDLY ACCUMULATING STORES .... WE HAVE BEEN WONDERFULLY SUPPLIED....

Sherman, with his mind on logistics, was preparing for total war.

NOVEMBER 1863–AUGUST 1864:
• STALEMATE EAST & WEST •

NOVEMBER 19, 1863

• President Lincoln, dedicating a battlefield as a national cemetery, delivers one of the greatest speeches in American history: the Gettysburg Address. He told the audience—and all Americans, across the ages, "…we here highly resolve that these dead shall not have died in vain—that this nation, under God, shall have a new birth of freedom—and that government of the people, by the people, for the people, shall not perish from the earth."

SPRING 1864

• The Union forces emerge from winter quarters and launch major offenses, but stubborn Confederate resistance slows their progress. The seemingly endless and fruitless carnage encourages peace movements in the North.

MARCH 9, 1864

• President Lincoln promotes Grant to the newly revived rank of Lieutenant General and places him in command of all Union armies. Sherman succeeds Grant as commander in the western theater.

MAY 4, 1864

• Grant launches his great assault on Lee's armies in Virginia in a series of clashes ranging from the Wilderness to Spotsylvania to Cold Harbor that will come to be known as the Forty Days. It is in effect one giant battle of attrition, during which Union forces suffer 50,000 overall casualties, and the smaller Confederate forces about 27,000.

MAY 7, 1864

• Sherman, coordinating his attack with Grant's assault on Lee's forces and moving simultaneously to apply maximum pressure on the Confederate forces, launches his own advance toward the rail center of Atlanta.

JUNE 1864

• Grant repeatedly shifts his forces in an effort to outflank Lee's army, but Lee's forces "conform" (move to stay with him). Lee is losing his freedom of movement. As Grant pushes ever closer to Richmond, Lee is forced to keep his troops between the Union ranks and his capital.

• Sherman advances slowly toward Atlanta. The campaign consists mainly of complex maneuvers and small engagements that give the false impression that Sherman is producing casualties but no real results. The larger fights likewise seem to accomplish little. However, the cumulative effective is very great. The Confederate forces are pushed back almost continuously.

JUNE 8, 1864

• Republicans nominate Lincoln for a second term.

JUNE 15, 1864

• Grant's troops miss a chance to capture Petersburg, and settle into siege positions around Richmond and Petersburg, a key rail hub serving the Confederate capital. This immobilizes Lee's army. The stalemate in Virginia will last nine months.

EARLY JULY 1864

• Sherman's forces commence a slow encirclement of Atlanta.

JULY 12, 1864

• Union troops arrive in Washington just in time to repel an invasion by a Rebel force led by Lieutenant General Jubal A. Early.

AUGUST 17, 1864

• Lincoln telegraphs Grant: I HAVE SEEN YOUR DISPATCH EXPRESSING YOUR UNWILLINGNESS TO BREAK YOUR HOLD WHERE YOU ARE. NEITHER AM I WILLING. HOLD ON WITH A BULLDOG GRIP, AND CHEW AND CHOKE AS MUCH AS POSSIBLE. The siege continues.

A gigantic explosion blows up a Confederate fort at besieged Petersburg. Union soldiers who had been miners before the war dug a long tunnel, filled an underground chamber with four tons of powder, and lit the fuse.

CHAPTER TWELVE

· TOTAL WAR ·

❖

The siege of Petersburg, gateway to Richmond, was beginning its 45th day on July 30, 1864, when a Union officer felt a "slight tremor of the earth for a second, then the rocking as of an earthquake." Next came a "tremendous blast" as a "vast column of earth and smoke shot upward" into the sky, "its dark sides flashing out sparks of fire." The column began to collapse and down came "showers of stones, broken timbers and blackened human limbs." Where once a Confederate fort had stood, there now was only a gaping hole and the bodies of 278 Confederate soldiers.

Technologically, the explosion that created the Crater—a hole about 200 feet long, 60 to 80 feet wide, and 30 feet deep—was a remarkable achievement. The Crater, now a cluster of grassy humps at Petersburg National

Copperheads threaten the Union in this 1863 cartoon.

Battlefield Park, is also a monument to the idea of total war—an idea that inspired the Crater as much as military planning did.

"Total war" is a label for a war that goes beyond the battlefield and beyond what people normally consider decent human behavior. Modern military historians trace the total war policy of World War II to the Civil War. When the Civil War began, men on both sides believed that it would be possible to wage war in a "chivalrous," or well-mannered, way. But Commander in Chief Lincoln soon came to realize the need for total war. Even the freeing of slaves in the Confederate states, which he ordered in the Emancipation Proclamation, was, in his view, a military decision based on the realization that the war extended far from the battlefields.

On April 24, 1863—two years into the war—Lincoln issued General Order No. 100, which said, "Military necessity admits of all direct destruction of life or limb of armed enemies, and of other persons whose destruction is incidentally unavoidable in the armed contests of the war; it allows…all destruction of property, and obstruction of the ways and channels of traffic, travel, or communication, and of all withholding of sustenance or means of life from the enemy…."

Lincoln does not seem to have known the details of the Crater operation. But by July 1864 he certainly knew that General Grant, who was by then commander of all Union armies, was doing whatever military necessity demanded to end the war. Both Grant and Lincoln were looking at another part of total war: politics as tied to warfare.

People were tired of the war and the long casualty lists usually transmitted by telegraph and published in the newspapers. A presidential election was coming in November, and military victories could help get Lincoln reelected. Grant, in search of such a victory, had taken so many men on a campaign to capture the Confederate capital that Washington was in danger. And so was Lincoln.

In early July 1864 raiding Confederates were on the outskirts of Washington. Soldiers left their hospital beds to limp to the forts surrounding the city, joining federal office workers preparing for a final, desperate defense while awaiting reinforcements from Grant. A Navy ship stood by on the Potomac to take Lincoln out of the city.

Grant sent troops to the rescue by steamboat. The reinforcements headed for Fort Stevens, about five miles from the White House. When they surged out of the fort to drive back the Confederates, Lincoln was there. He wanted to see for himself how his "soldiers repulse the invaders." He is the only President ever to be on a battlefield under enemy fire.

The Union troops drove back the Confederates, ending the threat, but nothing was going right for Grant in his campaign to take Richmond.

He was bogged down at Petersburg, a small town about 20 miles south of Richmond. Petersburg controlled the lifeline to the Confederate capital: two railroads that passed through the town and a third nearby. If Grant could get to those railroads, he could force the Confederate troops in Richmond to surrender or flee or starve. At the same time,

· EMANCIPATION PROCLAMATION ·

Lincoln fought the Civil War not to end slavery, but to save the Union. He hated slavery and wanted it to end. In August 1861, he issued a proclamation freeing slaves who were being used for war work by the Confederacy. In April 1862 he prohibited slavery in Washington, and in June 1862 he extended this prohibition to include the western territories.

Lincoln had to contend with many pro-Union politicians who were also pro-slavery. To explain his beliefs, Lincoln wrote an open letter to newspaper publisher Horace Greeley on August 22, 1862. "My paramount object in this struggle is to save the Union, and is not either to save or to destroy slavery," he said. "If I could save the Union without freeing any slave I would do it, and if I could save it by freeing all the slaves I would do it; and if I could save it by freeing some and leaving others alone I would also do that."

A devilish Lincoln plays the free-the-slaves card in a British cartoon that views the Emancipation Proclamation as an explosive move.

Lincoln wanted to impose "forcible abolition" only following a Union victory. He had to wait until after McClellan's defeat in the Peninsular Campaign and other military failures. He wanted to act from a strong military position not a weak one. His announcement finally came after the Battle of Antietam in September 1862, a victory of sorts. He said the Emancipation Proclamation would go into effect on January 1, 1863. The proclamation declared that "all persons held as slaves" within the Confederate states "are, and henceforward shall be free." So, by freeing all slaves in areas that were in rebellion, it did not free slaves in the loyal states.

The proclamation was primarily a military measure that Lincoln made as Commander in Chief. He freed slaves, not to make Northern abolitionists happy, but to hurt the Confederacy and the Southern economy. It also transformed Confederate slaves into Union soldiers and sailors. Another useful military effect was that it put the North on record as being against slavery. This made it all but impossible for Great Britain or France to intervene in the war because siding with the Confederacy would mean siding with slavery, which was outlawed in both countries. Left unsaid was the fact that, with slavery now clearly an issue, Southerners could no longer expect to somehow negotiate a surrender that would allow them to keep their slaves.

But the Proclamation went further still. It changed a war to save the Union into something more: a war to end slavery.

"The Dictator," an almost 9-ton Union mortar, hurled 218-pound shells at Petersburg during the siege.

Sherman was leading a campaign to capture another key rail center: Atlanta, Georgia. Victory at Richmond or Atlanta would help to reelect Lincoln in November 1864.

In Petersburg, the secret digging of a 510-foot tunnel that created the Crater had set in motion a grand plan meant to end the siege and doom Richmond. As soon as the underground super-mine went off, thousands of Union troops were to charge through the opening, overrun the Confederate lines, take Petersburg, and drive on to Richmond.

The digging and planting of the explosives was directed by Lieutenant Colonel Henry Pleasants, commanding officer of a Pennsylvania infantry regiment full of coal miners. Pleasants, a civil engineer before the war, had helped to dig a Pennsylvania railroad tunnel nearly a mile long. To produce the Petersburg tunnel, Pleasants had to figure a way not only to dig it but also to ventilate it. His

men hauled out 18,000 cubic feet of dirt (enough to fill a three-bedroom modern home from floor to ceiling), hid the dirt at night in a ravine, and covered the dirt with brush. They then put 8,000 pounds of gunpowder in a chamber directly under a Confederate fort and, at great risk, twice lit a fuse to detonate it.

The explosion blasted a wide gap in the Confederate line, but bungling Union officers had not planned properly for what to do next. As a result, they failed to get their men through the breach quickly and effectively. Many Union soldiers found themselves at the bottom of a pit, being fired down upon by Rebel soldiers.

The Confederates killed, wounded, or captured nearly 4,000 Union soldiers while losing about 1,500 men. Among the Union soldiers attacked in the Crater were many black troops. Those who survived the attack in the Crater were treated not as prisoners of war but as runaway

UNION AND LIBERTY!   AND   UNION AND SLAVERY!

This political cartoon suggests how postwar life in the Union will differ depending on whether Lincoln or McClellan is victorious.

slaves who were either returned to their masters or executed. The Confederacy did not recognize black troops as soldiers.

Such ruthless treatment of black soldiers had been a large part of the reason federal officials had stopped paroling prisoners. As a further response to such abuses, Lincoln issued General Order No. 233, threatening to punish Confederate prisoners for harm done to captured black Union soldiers. The threat, though rarely if ever carried out, had some effect on Rebel actions, and it was further evidence of the North's commitment to total war.

As the siege of Petersburg wore on, Lincoln feared that voter weariness with the war would lead to his defeat in November. On August 23, he wrote some words on a piece of paper and sealed it. "This morning, as for some days past," the document said, "it seems exceedingly probable that this Administration will not be re-elected. Then it will be my duty to so co-operate with the President-elect, as to save the Union between the election and the inauguration; as he will have secured his election on such ground that he can not possibly save it afterwards." He then asked each member of his Cabinet to sign the back of the document without reading it. They would be shown what they had signed, he said, after the election.

Lincoln knew that his chief opponent was a candidate advocating immediate peace negotiations, a continuation of slavery in the South, and a denial of the Emancipation Proclamation. The candidate was George B. McClellan, whom Lincoln had fired as commander of the Army of the Potomac in 1862.

Lincoln had little hope that McClellan, if elected, would listen to him or his Cabinet members in the time between the November election and the March Inauguration. As an added precaution, Lincoln secretly asked the well-known abolitionist and black leader Frederick

Douglass to develop a plan for helping as many slaves as possible to escape from Union-held territory in the South before election day. On August 29, Douglass gave Lincoln a plan that called for the President to appoint agents who would go to Union lines throughout the South, round up as many former slaves as possible, and help get them safely to Northern states.

Lincoln held off from carrying out the Douglass plan because suddenly he had a victory. On September 1, the Confederates evacuated Atlanta. Two days later Sherman telegraphed General in Chief Halleck in Washington: SO ATLANTA IS OURS, AND FAIRLY WON.

The first of the Union's hammer blows against the South had been the closing of Mobile Bay, shutting the last major port on the Gulf of Mexico and tightening the blockade. The second was the seizure of Atlanta and its vital rail connections, cutting major transportation links. Both of these were total war-style attacks—not against the Confederate army, but against the Confederate economy. The third hammer blow struck at the Southern food supply. It was Major General Philip Sheridan's August to October 1864 campaign in Virginia's Shenandoah Valley.

Back in July, Sheridan had defeated the Confederate raiders that had threatened Washington. Next, executing what in modern warfare would be called a scorched-earth campaign, he and his men drove off livestock and burned crops, barns, and mills in the valley to ensure that it would no longer be a food source for the enemy. "If a crow wants to fly down the Shenandoah, he must carry his provisions with him," Sheridan boasted. This was total war—quite literally with a vengeance.

By the fall of 1864, with desertions and battle casualties wearing down the Confederate army, few in the South believed that they could win the war on the battlefield. But total war included political warfare, and some Confederate leaders still thought that they could win the political war by defeating Lincoln on election day with the help of the Copperheads. To supporters, a Copperhead was a pro-peace, anti-Lincoln patriot who wore, as an emblem of freedom, the Indian head symbol cut from a copper penny. To foes, a Copperhead was a copperhead snake, dangerous and deceitful.

Major General Philip Sheridan doffs his hat as he leads a total-war mission: denying Shenandoah Valley harvests to Confederate soldiers.

army, secede from the Union, and form a new Northwest Confederacy, where slavery would be legal.

Lincoln, who had sources of intelligence that are still unknown, somehow learned about the conspiracy. To get a firsthand report, he ordered his trusted secretary John Hay to travel west to St. Louis, where he would be given a verbal report to relay to Lincoln. There would be nothing written down on paper. Union army officers in St. Louis told Hay the extent of the Copperhead conspiracy and gave him the name of its principal leader: former Ohio Congressman Clement Vallandigham.

Confederate agents operating out of pro-South Canada focused on allying with Copperheads in the Union Northwest (a region now made up of Missouri, Ohio, Illinois, and Indiana). Copperheads living in the Northwest, aided by the Confederacy, were to organize an

Vallandigham had been arrested by Union soldiers in 1863 for making treasonous statements. Lincoln, who had

A giant Majority carries Lincoln to victory in the 1864 election. A dunce burdens McClellan, who won only three states.

opposed his arrest, had ordered him banished to the Confederacy. He knew that imprisoning the Congressman would make the Copperhead a martyr. Vallandigham later slipped into Canada, where he joined other Confederate conspirators. Hay, back in Washington, told Lincoln that Vallandigham had returned to the United States and was urging Democrats to vote for McClellan. Lincoln decided not to risk a pre-election uprising by moving against the anti-war, pro-South fugitive.

Lincoln's shrewd decision worked. Throughout the North, newspapers told of the Copperhead Conspiracy, the treachery of Vallandigham, and McClellan's connections to the Copperheads. Republicans spread the word: McClellan was associated with treason while Lincoln was for winning the war. (In fact, McClellan denounced the Copperhead peace-

settlement idea and asserted that he would continue the war, promising to run it better than Lincoln did.)

Among Lincoln's worries about reelection was losing the "soldiers' vote." McClellan had a reputation for being admired by his men, no matter the outcome of the battles they fought under his command. And, for the first time, soldiers could vote by absentee ballot in several states. States that did not approve military absentee ballots did allow soldiers home on leave to vote.

The soldiers' vote for McClellan that Lincoln feared did not happen. Lincoln received 55 percent of the popular vote in November 1864, and his share of the soldiers' vote was estimated to be about 80 percent.

In March 1865, after his Inauguration, Lincoln met with Grant at City Point, Virginia, to begin the task of ending the war. Aboard the *River Queen*, Grant's steamboat headquarters on the James River near Richmond, Lincoln also talked with Major General Sherman, the conqueror of Atlanta.

Sherman firmly believed in total war, both in military and political terms. After taking Atlanta, Sherman had launched what became known as his March to the Sea. Following the example of Grant in the Vicksburg campaign, he wanted to let his soldiers live off the land, as they swept across Georgia and into South Carolina, taking whatever food was needed and destroying whatever would aid the enemy. Lincoln had ordered him to hold off until after the election. So Sherman had begun his campaign on November 12, continuing until he captured Columbia, South Carolina, on February 17, 1865.

Sherman believed that the Union was "not only fighting hostile armies, but a hostile people." He felt that he "must make old and young, rich and poor, feel the hard hand of war, as well as their organized armies." Looking back on his merciless long march across the South, he wrote, "I know that this recent movement of mine through Georgia has had a wonderful effect in this respect.

Thousands who had been deceived by their lying newspapers to believe that we were being whipped all the time now realize the truth, and have no appetite for a repetition of the same experience."

Sherman, denounced as a fiend by Southerners, was cheered on by Lincoln. Now, as Lincoln met day after day with Sherman and Grant at City Point, the focus was on the future, not the past. Both generals told their Commander in Chief that the war would soon end in a Southern surrender. But what would be the terms? Lincoln said he wanted most of all "to get the deluded men of the rebel armies disarmed and back to their homes…Let them once surrender and reach their homes, [and] they won't take up arms again.…I want no one punished.…We want those people to return to their allegiance to the Union and submit to the laws."

On the night of March 29, from the deck of the *River Queen*, Lincoln could hear the thundering artillery that signaled the start of Grant's final drive to charge through the maze of trenches at Petersburg. Grant's men succeeded in cutting the rail lines that were Lee's last supply line. It

Jubilant Richmond slaves, newly freed, cluster around President Lincoln as he rides through what had been the capital of the Confederacy.

was not the capture of trenches and positions but the wrecking of Lee's logistics that flushed his Army of Northern Virginia out of its fortifications. With no hope of getting food and ammunition to his hungry troops, Lee had no choice but to head as fast as he could toward another rail line along which he could evacuate his troops and link up with Confederate forces still in the field beyond Virginia.

On Sunday, April 2, General Robert E. Lee withdrew from Richmond and headed westward with one last desperate hope: He and his men would link up with Brigadier General Johnston's army in North Carolina and fight on from there.

The next morning, Lincoln boarded a Navy warship and, with his 12-year-old son Tad, headed up the James River to a dock in Richmond. Much of the city was on fire, and shells were exploding in the flaming ammunition warehouses on the waterfront. A startled Union officer saw "a crowd coming, headed by President Lincoln, who was walking with his usual long, careless stride, and looking about with an interested air and taking in everything." The officer saluted Lincoln and, at his request, took him to the home of Confederacy President Jefferson Davis, which had become Union army headquarters. Davis and his Cabinet had fled the city the day before.

After exploring the house and sitting in what he hoped was Davis's chair, Lincoln met with Union and Confederate officials. Union officers asked for orders about what they "should do in regard to the conquered people." Lincoln gave this reply: "If I were in your place, I'd let 'em up easy, let 'em up easy."

Black men, women, and children, who had been slaves the day before, now were free. They gathered around Lincoln in the streets, laughing and crying. One black man fell to his knees. "Don't kneel to me," Lincoln said. "That is not right. You must kneel to God only, and thank Him for the liberty you will enjoy hereafter." Warned that his life was in danger in Richmond, Lincoln said, "I cannot bring myself to believe that any human being lives who would do me any harm."

Meanwhile, Lee's 35,000 men were heading west toward Amelia Court House, where tens of thousands of rations were waiting in railroad boxcars. But when the Confederates arrived, they discovered the boxcars were full of ammunition not rations. Lee telegraphed to Lynchburg and Danville, two other railroad stops with storage depots, asking for 200,000 rations. Union wiretappers intercepted the message, gaining one last bit of vital intelligence: Lee was out of food. The last moves of Lee's army were toward rail-carried supplies, and his final defeat was speeded

· JUNETEENTH ·

The joyous news about the Emancipation Proclamation spread quickly through most of the North and followed in the wake of Union victories throughout the South. But word about the Proclamation did not reach the 250,000 slaves in Texas until June 19, 1865. That was when Major General Gordon Granger read the Proclamation after arriving in Galveston with Union troops. The news spread quickly through the state.

Juneteenth, as the day of the reading was called, became an annual day of celebration. Black organizations raised money to buy land for Juneteenth events, and many of the sites became known as Emancipation Parks. In 1979, the day was made an official state holiday in Texas. Today, 28 other states recognize it as a holiday.

After the Proclamation, slavery was still legal in Delaware, Kentucky, Missouri, Maryland, and New Jersey. Abolishing slavery throughout the nation required a Constitutional amendment. The 13th Amendment, which prohibits slavery, was proposed in January 1865 and ratified (approved) by a two-thirds vote of Congress. In December 1865 it was approved by three-fourths of the states (including 8 of the 11 former Confederate states). In 1995 Mississippi was the last former Confederate state to approve it.

The 14th Amendment, which was ratified in 1868, guarantees full Constitutional rights to all citizens, including African Americans. The 15th Amendment, which gives black men the right to vote, was ratified in 1870. It was not until the 19th Amendment was ratified in 1920 that the Constitution gave American women the right to vote.

A simple device allowed operators to test or tap wires.

by the interception of a telegraph message.

The pursuing Union army maneuvered to keep Lee from heading toward North Carolina, forcing him westward across the Appomattox River. I SEE NO ESCAPE FOR LEE, Major General Philip Sheridan wired Grant. In another message to Grant, Sheridan told of taking 6,000 prisoners and most of Lee's wagon train. IF THE THING IS PRESSED, Sheridan telegraphed, I THINK LEE WILL SURRENDER.

Lincoln saw the message. On the morning of April 7, he wired Grant:....LET THE THING BE PRESSED. Later that day, under a white flag carried through Confederate lines, Grant sent a note to Lee, citing "the hopelessness of further resistance." The note led to a meeting on April 9 between Grant and Lee in a house in the village of Appomattox Court House, Virginia.

There, the two generals talked for about two and a half hours. Grant—following Lincoln's order that he wanted "no one punished"—wrote these terms: "...each

officer and man will be allowed to return to his home, not to be disturbed by the United States authorities so long as they observe their paroles, and the laws in force where they may reside." Lee, satisfied that he and his men would not be tried as traitors, agreed to the terms and signed the document. There was still Johnston's surrender to come shortly in North Carolina. But the two generals at Appomattox had ended the Civil War.

About a week later, hours before his assassination, Lincoln was asked about the possibility of Rebel leaders escaping. He said, "Well, I should not be sorry to see them out of the country, but I should be for following them up pretty close to make sure of their going....I hope there will be no persecution, no bloody work after the war is over. No one need expect me to take any part in hanging or killing these men, even the worst of them. Frighten them out of the country; open the gates; let down the bars." He gestured

General Robert E. Lee (seated at left) surrenders to General Ulysses S. Grant (seated at right center) in the parlor of Wilmer McLean's home in Appomattox Court House on April 9, 1865.

with his hands and said, "Shoo; scare them off....enough lives have been sacrificed."

Grant's terms of surrender echoed the words that had been handed down by Abraham Lincoln in his second Inaugural Address, when he had envisioned the end of the war that he had commanded: "With malice toward none, with charity for all, with firmness in the right as God gives us to see the right, let us strive…to do all which may achieve and cherish a just and lasting peace among ourselves and with all nations."

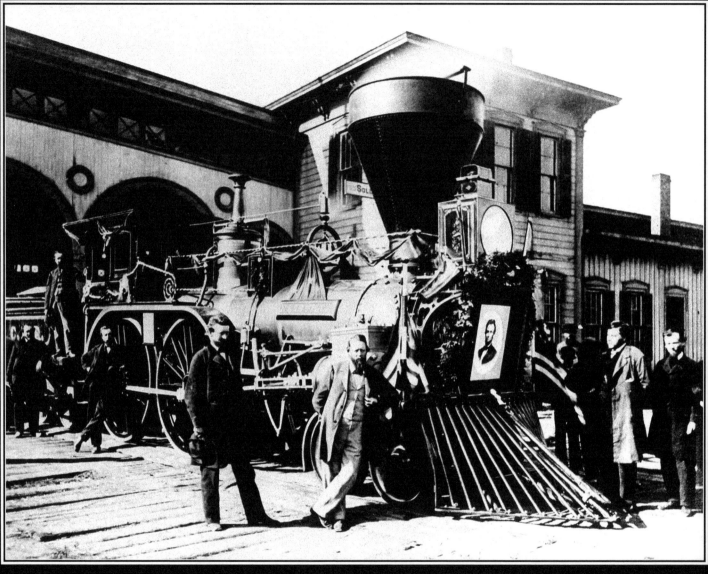

Abraham Lincoln's funeral train carried the body of the assassinated President, who had made railroads a weapon of war. Mourners gathered at hundreds of communities along the way, as the train traveled from Washington to Springfield, Illinois.

· A LEGACY BEYOND THE BATTLEFIELD ·

On the morning of April 15, 1865, just six days after the surrender at Appomattox, Secretary of War Edwin M. Stanton dictated a telegram to be sent from the War Department telegraph office that President Lincoln had frequented so often: ABRAHAM LINCOLN DIED THIS MORNING AT TWENTY-TWO MINUTES AFTER SEVEN O'CLOCK.

The night before, John Wilkes Booth, a famous actor and Southern sympathizer, had slipped into Ford's Theater in Washington, opened the door to the box where President and Mrs. Lincoln were watching a play, and shot the President in the back of the head.

A grieving nation made the assassinated President a martyr of the war that he had led. But there was more to Lincoln's legacy. His zealous interest in invention and

Lincoln is assassinated by John Wilkes Booth at Ford's Theater.

technology went beyond weapons and battle to a vision of a future America that he helped to create.

In the midst of the war, Lincoln signed the Pacific Railway Act for the building of a transcontinental railroad, an idea that had been discussed since 1853. At Promontory Point, Utah, on May 10, 1869, a golden spike was hammered home to signify the completion of a railroad that linked East and West. A telegram instantly was sent to President Ulysses S. Grant: WE HAVE THE HONOR TO REPORT THAT THE LAST RAIL IS LAID, THE LAST SPIKE IS DRIVEN. THE PACIFIC RAILROAD IS FINISHED.

The Homestead Act, vetoed by Lincoln's predecessor, President James Buchanan, was championed and signed by Lincoln in the midst of the war with these words: "So that every poor man may have a home." The law gave each

Bricks of sod made this cow-topped house on land granted by the Homestead Act,
signed by Lincoln "so that every poor man may have a home."

land to be used as sites for colleges. More than 70 land grant colleges were established under this act. Many a peacetime President has failed to achieve anywhere near as many important advances and reforms. Lincoln did it all, and much more, in the midst of war.

While Lincoln was being Commander in Chief, he was also the President, watching over events that were taking place on land far from the battlefields. Lincoln brought the nation together not only by leading the Union to victory in the Civil War but also by opening a new way westward, developing America's farming heartland and planting colleges where none had been before.

homesteader—man or woman—160 acres of undeveloped land. Eventually, the act would put homes and farms and ranches on 270 million acres.

Another idea vetoed by President Buchanan became, under Lincoln, the Land Grant Act of 1862, which gave each Union state—and after the war each former Confederate state—vast tracts of federally controlled

To the end of his life, and well beyond, his vision of the benefits of progress and technology brought "new and useful things" to the nation.

Survivors of the Army of the Potomac march down Pennsylvania Avenue in the Grand Review, celebrating the end of the Civil War. White House columns are swathed in black, mourning the assassinated President.

BIBLIOGRAPHY

BOOKS

Official Records of the Union and Confederate Navies in the War of the Rebellion, Volumes: Series I, 1–27; Series II, 1–3, Washington, DC: Govt. Print. Office, 1894–1922. (Abbreviated *ORN;* see note in Online Resources section.)

The War of the Rebellion: A Compilation of the Official Records of the Union and Confederate Armies, Volumes: Series I, 1–53; Series II, 1–8; Series III, 1–5; Series IV, 1–4, Washington, DC: Govt. Print. Office, 1880–1901. (Abbreviated *OR;* see note in Online Resources section.)

Allen, Thomas B. *The Blue and the Gray.* Washington, DC: National Geographic Society, 1993.

Axelrod, Alan. *The War Between the Spies: A History of Espionage During the American Civil War.* NY: Atlantic Monthly Press, 1992.

_____. *Lincoln's Last Night: Abraham Lincoln, John Wilkes Booth, and the Last 36 Hours Before the Assassination.* NY: Chamberlain Bros. (Penguin Group), 2005.

Bates, David Homer. *Lincoln in the Telegraph Office.* NY: The Century Co., 1907.

Blackman, Ann. *Wild Rose: Rose O'Neale Greenhow, Civil War Spy: A True Story.* NY: Random House, 2005.

Bruce, Robert V. *Lincoln and the Tools of War.* Urbana and Chicago, IL: University of Illinois Press, 1956.

Bulloch, James D. *The Secret Service of the Confederate States in Europe: or How the Confederate Cruisers Were Equipped.* London, England: Richard Bentley & Son, 1883; Reprinted NY: Random House (Modern Library War Series), 2001.

Catton, Bruce. *A Stillness at Appomattox.* NY: Simon & Schuster, 1953.

_____. *American Heritage Pictorial History of the Civil War.* NY: American Heritage Publishing Co., 1960.

Cochran, Hamilton. *Blockade Runners of the Confederacy.* NY: Bobbs-Merrill, 1958.

Coffin, Charles Carleton. *Freedom Triumphant: The Fourth Period of the War of the Rebellion.* NY: Harper & Brothers, 1890.

Crouch, Tom D. *The Eagle Aloft: Two Centuries of the Balloon in America.* Washington, DC: Smithsonian Press, 1983.

deKay, James Tertius. *Monitor.* NY: Walker, 1997.

Donald, David Herbert. *Lincoln.* NY: Simon & Schuster, 1995.

Evans, Charles M. *War of the Aeronauts: A History of Ballooning in the Civil War.* Mechanicsburg, PA: Stackpole Books, 2002.

Foote, Shelby. *The Civil War: A Narrative, Volume 1: Fort Sumter to Perryville.* NY: Random House, 1958.

_____. *The Civil War: A Narrative, Volume 2: Fredericksburg to Meridian.* NY: Random House, 1963.

_____. *The Civil War: A Narrative, Volume 3: Red River to Appomattox.* NY: Random House, 1974.

Fowler, Jr., William M. *Under Two Flags: The American Navy in the Civil War.* NY: W.W. Norton, 1990.

Gallman, J. Matthew (editor). *The Civil War Chronicle.* NY: Crown Publishers (Random House), 2000.

Haydon, F. Stansbury. *Military Ballooning During the Early Civil War.* Baltimore, MD: Johns Hopkins University Press, 2000.

Howarth, Stephen. *To Shining Sea.* NY: Random House, 1991.

Jones, Virgil Carrington. *The Civil War at Sea: Volume One: The Blockaders.* NY: Holt, Reinhart Winston, 1960.
_____. *The Civil War at Sea: Volume Two: The River War.* NY: Holt, Rinehart Winston, 1961.
_____. *The Civil War at Sea: Volume Three: The Final Effort.* NY: Holt, Rinehart Winston, 1962.

Luraghi, Rainondo. *A History of the Confederate Navy.* Annapolis, MD: Naval Institute Press, 1996.

Marvel, William (editor). *The Monitor Chronicles: One Sailor's Account—Today's Campaign to Recover the Civil War Wreck.* NY: Simon & Schuster, 2000.

McPherson, James M. *Battle Cry of Freedom: The Civil War Era.* NY: Oxford University Press, 1988.

Milligan, John D. *Gunboats Down the Mississippi.* Annapolis, MD: Naval Institute Press, 1965.

Ross, Charles D. *Trial By Fire: Science, Technology, and the Civil War.* Shippensburg, PA: White Mane Books, 2000.

Scharf, J. Thomas. *History of the Confederate States Navy.* NY: Rogers & Sherwood, 1887.

Sears, Stephen W. *To the Gates of Richmond: The Peninsular Campaign.* NY: Ticknor & Fields, 1992.

Soderberg, Susan Cooke. *A Guide to Civil War Sites in Maryland: Blue and Gray in a Border State.* Shippensburg, PA: White Mane Books, 1998.

Stokesbury, James L. *A Short History of the Civil War.* NY: William Morrow, 1995.

Sullivan, George. *The Civil War at Sea.* Brookfield, CT: Twenty-First Century Books, 2001.

Tidwell, William A. *April '65: Confederate Covert Action in the American Civil War.* Kent, OH: Kent State University Press, 1995.

Weber, Jennifer L. *Copperheads: The Rise and Fall of Lincoln's Opponents in the North.* NY: Oxford University Press, 2006.

Wise, Stephen R. *Lifeline of the Confederacy: Blockade Running During the Civil War.* Columbia, SC: University of South Carolina Press, 1988.

ONLINE RESOURCES

Note: A list of links to the online resources below, updated links to new Web sites, and other Web sites of interest for specific topics as well as additional information about the high-tech war and more information on many Civil War topics can be found at this book's Web site: www.mrlincolnshightechwar.com

Mr. Lincoln's High-Tech War was written at the dawn of a golden age for finding things out. The amount of information available on the Internet is utterly overwhelming. Here are a few of the most valuable resources for studying the Civil War. Note that the addresses and contents of Web sites are subject to change. Those listed below are not only of especially high value for general research into the Civil War but also likely to remain available for the foreseeable future.

The War of the Rebellion: A Compilation of the Official Records of the Union and Confederate Armies, and Official Records of the Union and Confederate Navies in the War of the Rebellion are commonly referred to as the Official Records and Official Records, Navy. They are often abbreviated as OR and ORN. They represent the primary sources for virtually any research into the Civil War. The 70 volumes of the OR and ORN are available in searchable form at Cornell University's Making of America site [http://cdl.library.cornell.edu/moa/browse.monographs/waro.html for the OR; http://cdl.library.cornell.edu/moa/browse.monographs/ofre.html for the ORN]. These resources were invaluable in the writing of Mr. Lincoln's High-Tech War. (Many other texts are available at the Making of America home site [http://cdl.library.cornell.edu/moa/moa_browse.html], including 19th-century editions of Scientific American and Harper's Monthly. The pages of the original volumes can be displayed as facsimiles or as plain text, though the conversion to text is sometimes unreliable, and the full text of the OR and ORN is searchable.) The OR is available as searchable text at http://ehistory.osu.edu/osu/sources/records/ along with the Atlas to Accompany the Official Records, which includes many spectacular maps as well as diagrams of weapons, uniforms, equipment, and flags used in the war.

The Dictionary of American Naval Fighting Ships. There are many online versions of DANFS, but the definitive one, maintained by the U.S. Navy Historical Society, is at http://history.navy.mil/danfs/index.html. It provides histories of virtually every U.S. and Confederate ship, along with a vast selection of photographs and other images and links to accounts of important battles and actions.

The Lincoln Log: a day-to-day record of Lincoln's life, available at www.thelincolnlog.org, provides a day-by-day, and sometimes hour-by-hour account of Lincoln's life. Searchable by date and keyword, it provides citations and links to many other resources. The Collected Works of Abraham Lincoln with searchable text is available at http://quod.lib.umich.edu/l/lincoln/. Mr. Lincoln's White House at http://www.mrlincolnswhitehouse.org/ provides maps, diagrams, histories, and a great deal more.

The full text of all of Harper's Weekly for the war years is available at http://www.sonofthesouth.net/.

Here are some other sites on specific topics. The Central Intelligence Agency offers a Web site on intelligence in the Civil War at https://www.cia.gov/library/publications/additional-publications/civil-war/index.html. The Monitor Center at http://www.monitorcenter.org provides a look at many aspects of the U.S.S. Monitor and the C.S.S. Virginia. The privately run site www.cssvirginia.org is a good source as well. A personal Web page on "Ironclads and Blockade Runners of the Civil War" is at http://www.wideopenwest.com/~jenkins/ironclads/ironclad.htm. The Friends of the Hunley site at http://www.hunley.org details the doomed sub's career along with information on her rediscovery, recovery, and ongoing reconstruction—and a Hunley simulator. See also http://home.att.net/~JVNautilus/Hunley/reconstruction.html for a fascinating ongoing effort to do a digital reconstruction of the Hunley.

Many 19th-century books pertaining to the Civil War have been placed online as text or in scans of the original book's pages. See archive.org, books.google.com, and www.gutenberg.org. Most texts are downloadable in one form or another; others must be viewed online.

QUOTE SOURCES

Note: Full bibliographic information is listed only for the first reference or for sources not listed in the Bibliography or in Online Resources. If an author has written more than one book, the title referred to is in parentheses. The notation "OR" refers to The War of the Rebellion: A Compilation of the Official Records of the Union and Confederate Armies and "ORN" refers to Official Records of the Union and Confederate Navies in the War of the Rebellion (see note in Online Resources).

PROLOGUE: THE SPIRIT OF INVENTION
p. 8 "secured to…useful things." "Lecture on Discoveries and Inventions," presented by Abraham Lincoln on February 11, 1859, in Jacksonville, Illinois, quoted in Lincoln, Speeches and Writings, Volume 2, 1859–1861, p.12, Library of America.

SITUATION REPORT 1850-1860
p. 9 (1857) "had no…to respect." New York Times, November 27, 1900; (1858) "A house…half free." Collected Works of Abraham Lincoln, 1953, Volume 2, circa p. 461 as cited at http://quod.lib.umich.edu/l/lincoln/; (1859) "the crimes…with Blood." http://www.wvculture.org/History/jnobrown.html.

CHAPTER 1: LINCOLN'S SECRET TRAIN
p. 13 "Civil war…the sun." Gallman, p. 23; p. 14 PLUMS…SAFELY. http://reference.findtarget.com/search/Baltimore%20Plot/; p. 15 "very first…hands" http://www.mrlincolnswhitehouse.org/inside.asp?ID=153&subjectID=2; "an attempt…will be made." McPherson, p. 272.

CHAPTER 2: LINCOLN TAKES COMMAND
p. 18 "pay no…drop him." Report of Col. Edward F. Jones, Sixth Massachusetts Militia, April 22, 1861 http://civilwarhome.com/jones.htm; "You would….and severely." http://www.abrahamlincolnsclassroom.org/Library/newsletter.asp?ID=108&CRLI=156; p. 19 lyrics of "Maryland! My Maryland!" http://www.50states.com/songs/maryland.htm; p. 20 "The White House….East Room." Hay diary, April 18, 1861, quoted on p. 1 of Lincoln and the Civil War in the Diaries and Letters of John Hay, edited by Tyler Dennett, De Capo Press, NY, 1988; "it is not….every step." The Lincoln Log, April 18, 1861; "Why don't…come?" Donald, p. 298; p. 21 "The engine….run her." Butler's Book, by Benjamin Butler, A.M. Thayer & Co, Boston, 1892, p. 202.

CHAPTER 3: THE ANACONDA PLAN
p. 27 "until the organization….of any kind." Scharf, 1894, p. 17.

CHAPTER 4: LEARNING WAR
p.30 "My boy!…should be?" "Henry B. Whittington diary", http://www.alexandria.lib.va.us/lhsc_online_exhibits/cwpix/cwpix.html; "could bring…plan." http://www.mrlincolnswhitehouse.org/inside.asp?ID=39&subjectID=2; "The President…United States." U.S. Constitution, Article 2, Section 2, paragraph 1; p. 31 "these army matters," The Sword of Lincoln: The Army of the Potomac, by Jeffry D. Wert, Simon & Schuster, NY, 2005, p. 55; p. 33 "You are green…green alike." http://www.itd.nps.gov/cwss/battles_trans.htm; p.36 OUR ARMY IS RETREATING, Bates, p. 91; THE DAY…THIS ARMY, Donald, p. 307; p. 37 WAR DEPARTMENT….BE SHOT. Ibid., p. 93; "Let the volunteer….will permit." Collected Works of Abraham Lincoln, 1953, Volume 4, circa p. 457 as cited at http://quod.lib.umich.edu/l/lincoln/.

CHAPTER 5: RIDING THE WINDS OF BATTLE
p. 39 SIR: THIS POINT….COUNTRY, Evans, p. 71; p. 40 "My troubles….red tape." Ibid., p. 87; p. 45 "If McClellan...borrow it for a while." http://www.askoxford.com/worldofwords/quotations/quotefrom/Lincoln/; pp. 46–47 "Does not your plan….by mine?" "The Abraham Lincoln Papers"

at the Library of Congress http://memory.loc.gov/cgi-bin/query/r?ammem/mal:@field(DOCID +@lit(d1434200)); p. 48 "[i]t may be safely…. Professor Lowe." Crouch, p. 391; p. 49 "I have never…sight." Evans, p. 295.

CHAPTER 6: THE IRONCLADS
p. 53 "a good deal…something in it." deKay, p. 76; p. 58 "[W]e thought… for repair." McPherson, p. 376; "an immense…between ironclads." *Dictionary of American Naval Fighting Ships*, Monitor Entry; p. 62 THE CONGRESS…WILL BE TAKEN. *ORN*. Series I, Vol. 7, pp. 4–5; "will destroy…before we leave this room." See article by Gideon Welles from volume "Annals of the War" as published at http://www.civilwarhome.com/monitor.htm; "[W]e thought….between ironclads." *ORN*. Series I, Vol. 7, p. 53; p. 65 "[H]is Excellency….coaling." *ORN*, Series I, Vol. 7, p. 340.

CHAPTER 7: RUNNERS & RAIDERS
p. 69 "[W]e do not….fired upon." "Richmond's Bread Riot," *New York Times*, April 30, 1889; "Our slaves…his rights." McPherson, pp. 92–93; p. 70 "your system…itself." Foote, Volume 2, p. 578; p. 72 "to equip, furnish, or arm." Queen's Proclamation of May 13, 1861, quoted in "The American Conflict: Privateering and the Blockade— Her Majesty's Subjects and the American War," *New York Times*, May 28, 1861.

CHAPTER 8: OLD WAR, NEW WAR
p. 76 "See what….more so." http://www.nps.gov/vick/historyculture/troops-in-the-campaign-siege-and-defense-of-vicksburg.htm; "the nail head….together," http://americancivilwar.com/vicks.html; p. 77 "When this….the enemy." *Personal Memoirs of Ulysses S. Grant, Two Volumes in One*, University of Nebraska Press, 1996, p. 284; p. 79 "The soldiers….in the other." *Iowa in War Times*, by Samuel Hawkins Marshall Byers, W.D. Condit & Co., 1888, p. 230; p. 80 [TO] HON. GIDEON WELLES….REAR-ADMIRAL. *ORN*, Series I, Vol. 25, p. 103; "The Father…to the sea." Letter from Abraham Lincoln to James C. Conkling, August 26, 1863 *Collected Works of Abraham Lincoln*, Vol 6, pp. 406–410; p. 81 "Should the belief….bringing about." Foote, Vol. 2, p. 442; "Let him…but yesterday." *The Atlantic Monthly*, Volume 12, No. 69, July, 1863; p. 83 "General Lee to the rear!" http://www.civilwarhome.com/leetorear.htm; p. 84 "Filth, poor drainage…horror." http://www.civilwarhome.com/prisoners.htm; "the arithmetic," Foote, Vol. 2, p. 436; p. 85 "You cannot fill….cannot afford." Foote, Vol. 2, p. 578.

CHAPTER 9: SLOW MARCH TO RAPID FIRE
p. 87 "Well, you….a steadier nerve." Bruce, p. 263; p. 91 "At the distance…it out." *Personal Memoirs of Ulysses S. Grant*, p. 60; p. 97 "a great evil….all troops." Bruce, p. 69; p. 99 "insisting…by the Government." Ibid., p. 69; p. 100 "to the front….blaze away." Ibid., p. 105; p. 101 "I think the Johnnys…the week." *Civil War Small Arms*, by Bertram Barnett, Gettysburg National Military Park at http://www.nps.gov/archive/gett/soldierlife/webguns.htm.

CHAPTER 10: THE HOMEMADE NAVY
pp. 105–106 "Inequality of numbers….to first cost." "The Confederate Naval Buildup," by David G. Surdam, *Naval War College Review*, Winter, 2001, at http://findarticles.com/p/articles/mi_moJIW/is_1_54/ai75762216; p. 106 "ships that can….our enemy." Luraghi, p. 92.

CHAPTER 11: RAILS & WIRES AT WAR
p. 110 "stunned and confused…head." Donald, p. 457; "I will bet…in five days." Ibid., p. 458; p. 111 "introduced a new…the war." *Rescue by Rail: Troop Transfer and the Civil War in the West, 1863*, by Roger Pickenpaugh, University of Nebraska Press, 1998, p. 20; "take possession….all." Ibid., pp. 20–21; p. 113 "seen the most….beanpoles and cornstalks." Bruce, p. 215; p. 113 "cause Sherman…tunnels." *The Northern Railroads in the Civil War, 1861–1865*, by Thomas Weber,

Indiana University Press, 1999, p. 204; "The Cracker Line…boys!" http://www.civilwarhome.com/crackerline.htm; p. 116 THE RECENT….THE ARMY. *Report of the Joint Committee on the Conduct of the War (1865)*, Vol. I, p. 226, telegram addressed to General Daniel Butterfield; WHAT HATH…WROUGHT? http://memory.loc.gov/ammem/today/may24.html; p. 117 WASHINGTON, D.C.….BATES. Bates, p. 56; uncoded message, Ibid., p. 55; p. 120 "Is there not something under the blotter?" Ibid., pp. 94–96; "much obliged….own game." *ORN*, Series I, Vol. 25, p. 474; MY RAILROADS….SUPPLIED. *OR*, Series I, Vol. 38, Part Five, p. 123.

SITUATION REPORT NOVEMBER 1863–AUGUST 1864
p. 121 (August 17, 1864) "I HAVE SEEN….POSSIBLE. Foote, Vol 3, p. 549.

CHAPTER 12: TOTAL WAR
p. 123 "slight tremor…human limbs." *Army of Northern Virginia Memorial Volume*, compiled by Rev. J. William Jones, D.D., published by J.W. Randolph and English, Richmond, VA, 1880, p. 153; pp. 123–124 "Military necessity;…from the enemy." "Laws of War: General Orders No. 100; Instructions for the Government of Armies of the United States in the Field," prepared by Francis Lieber, promulgated as General Orders No. 100 by President Lincoln, 24 April 1863, online at http://www.yale.edu/lawweb/avalon/lieber.htm#sec1; p. 124 "soldiers repulse the invaders." *The Every-day Life of Abraham Lincoln*, Francis Fisher Browne (editor), 1887; reprint 1995 University of Nebraska Press, p. 662; p. 125 "My paramount….do that." *Collected Works of Abraham Lincoln*, 1953, Volume 5, circa p. 388 as cited at http://quod.lib.umich.edu/l/lincoln/; p. 127 "This morning,…afterwards." Memorandum Concerning His [Lincoln's] Probable Failure of Re-election, Aug. 23, 1864, *Collected Works of Abraham Lincoln*, Vol 7, p. 514 as shown online at http://quod.lib.umich.edu/l/lincoln/; p. 128 SO ATLANTA…FAIRLY WON. *OR*, Series I, Vol. 38, Part Five, p. 777; "If a crow wants to fly…with him." http://www.civil-war-battles.com/People/general-philipsheridan; p. 131 "not only fighting….the same experience." Message to Major General H. W. Halleck, December 24, 1864, quoted in "Nothing But Their Eyes to Weep With," *New York Times*, June 13, 1915; "to get the deluded men….submit to the laws." Donald, p. 574; p. 132 "a crowd coming….taking in everything." http://www.eyewitnesstohistory.com/richmond.htm; pp. 132–133 "should do….conquered people." *Abraham Lincoln: The War Years*, by Carl Sandburg, Harcourt Brace & Company, New York, 1939, p. 179; p. 133 "If I…up easy." http://www.eyewitnesstohistory.com/richmond.htm; "Don't kneel to me….enjoy hereafter." *April 1865, The Month that Saved America*, by Jay Winik, Harper, NY, p. 119; "I cannot bring myself to believe that any human being lives who would do me any harm." Donald, p. 577; p. 134 I SEE NO ESCAPE FOR LEE. *OR*, Series I, Vol. 46, Part Three, p. 582; IF THE THING….LET THE THING BE PRESSED. Foote, Vol. 3, pp. 903–904; "the hopelessness of further resistance." http://www.historynet.com/lieutenant-colonel-horace-c-porter-eyewitness-to-the-surrender-at-appomattox.htm; "each officer…reside." http://www.us-civilwar.com/appomattox.htm; pp. 134–135 "Well, I should not….have been sacrificed." Foote, Vol. 3, pp. 975–976; p. 135 "With malice toward none….with all nations." http://www.yale.edu/lawweb/avalon/presiden/inaug/lincoln2.htm.

EPILOGUE: A LEGACY BEYOND THE BATTLEFIELD
Page 137 ABRAHAM LINCOLN DIED…SEVEN O'CLOCK. *OR* Series I, Vol. 46, Part 3, p. 781; WE HAVE…FINISHED. http://cprr.org/Museum/Done!.html; "So that every poor man may have a home." *Abraham Lincoln: Complete Works Comprising his Speeches, Letters, State Papers, and Miscellaneous Writings*, edited by John G. Nicolay & John Hay, published by The Century Co., NY, 1907, p. 676; p. 138 "new and useful things," see source for page 8.

Founded in 1888, the National Geographic Society is one of the largest nonprofit scientific and educational organizations in the world. It reaches more than 285 million people worldwide each month through its official journal, NATIONAL GEOGRAPHIC, and its four other magazines; the National Geographic Channel; television documentaries; radio programs; films; books; videos and DVDs; maps; and interactive media. National Geographic has funded more than 8,000 scientific research projects and supports an education program combating geographic illiteracy.

For more information, please call 1-800-NGS LINE (647-5463) or write to the following address:

National Geographic Society
1145 17th Street N.W.
Washington, D.C. 20036-4688
U.S.A.

Visit us online at www.nationalgeographic.com /books